HISTORY of CHILDREN'S COSTUME

MARION SICHEL

Chelsea House Publishers
New York
Philadelphia

Published in the USA by
Chelsea House Publishers.
Printed and bound in the USA.

3 5 7 9 8 6 4 2

ISBN 1-55546-751-2

Contents

Introduction 3

The Classical Influence 4
    Ancient Greek dress 4
    Ancient Roman dress 4

The Early Britons 7
    The Roman period 7
    The Anglo-Saxon period 7
    The Norman period 8

The Twelfth Century 9

The Thirteenth Century 11

The Fourteenth Century 12

The Fifteenth Century 14

The Sixteenth Century 18

The Seventeenth Century 26

The Eighteenth Century 32

The Nineteenth Century 39

The Twentieth Century 58

Glossary of Terms 69

Bibliography 71

Index 72

Introduction

A book of this length can in no way be a complete history of children's clothes in Britain but I have set out to give a good general survey beginning with the Classical influence of Greece and Rome. The Anglo-Saxons copied the dress of the Romans in Britain, and the Crusaders returning from the East introduced to Western civilisation another and more sophisticated way of dress. There is, however, very scant information available until the time of the Norman conquest in 1066. The Bayeux Tapestry shows Norman clothing, as do many illustrated manuscripts, but because children were, in the main, dressed as adults, the information to be found specifically for them is very scarce.

Until the eighteenth century children's costume was scaled down replicas of adult dress, slightly less formal, with just a few adaptions and additions such as aprons and leading strings, but nevertheless restricting the movement of the child.

In our generation, when children have so much freedom, it is strange to think that as recently as the eighteenth century how restricted they were, not only in dress but also in upbringing. Even when they had escaped from the tightly laced bodices and long cumbersome coats into the more graceful dress worn by the end of the century, parental strictness remained.

One of the greatest influences in freeing children from these restricting clothes was John Locke (1632-1704), a philosopher. He was followed by the French author and philosopher Jean Jacques Rousseau (1712-1778), who was concerned with children's education. He did not believe that children should be just replicas of their parents, but individuals with their own demands, one of these being able to play and have freedom of movement in their clothes, which was obviously an impossibility whilst they were being dressed as miniature adults. Rousseau had to flee to England because of his radical ideas, but it took almost one hundred years for them to win acceptance.

The dress reform did however gain for the children a short respite, their fashions becoming less artificial and stiff, with simpler and looser garments; but by the 1830s children's clothes once again became very affected and had all the fashionable characteristics of the styles of their elders.

The nineteenth century, however, did not see complete liberation from the cumbersome dress, yet from the 1850s fashion magazines showed clothes specifically designed for children.

It was not until the twentieth century that light and practical clothes for children were universally accepted. Although a special market was inaugurated, the trends and fashions often had much in common with those of the adults.

The Classical Influence

The short tunics were made of squares of material joined together

Young boy in a toga draped in such a way that the folds in the front were often used as pockets. Around the neck is seen a bulla which was a small hollow ball worn by the wealthier citizens. The sandals were basically a sole held on with leather cross straps

Ancient Greek dress

Greek costume relied mainly on the art of drapery. The basic garment for boys and girls was a tunic called a *chiton* made of a single piece of material gathered at the shoulders with ornamental clasps, sometimes so folded as to form a kind of sleeve. Belts or cords allowed the material to be bloused or pleated. The boys usually wore their chiton shorter than the girls. A *peplum*, which was a long rectangular piece of cloth, was sometimes worn over the chiton. This was fastened at the shoulders, falling mainly to one side.

Young girls gathered their hair at the back with ribbons or tied it in a knot at the top of the head. Ornamental and jewelled hair decorations were very popular.

Boys often tucked their longish hair under a band that they wore around their heads.

Cloaks known as *himatia* were worn long or short and wide, and they were draped so that they could also be used as head coverings. The borders were usually decorated with patterns made from the popular 'key' design.

Ancient Roman dress

Roman tunics were very similar to those of the Greek chitons, except that Roman drapery was more pleated and fuller, with bloused effects also achieved with the use of belts.

For the girls two tunics and a veil were not unusual, worn under a cloak known as a *palla*, similar to the Greek himation.

Boys wore *togas*. The length of these was usually twice the height of the child; they were folded in half and pleated from the shoulders around the body. Basically, Roman costume derived directly from the Greek.

Toys

Throughout history most toys have appeared again and again, modified to suit their own epoch.

From Greek and Roman times animal shapes have been popular as playthings. They were made into toys and rattles. Dolls were also known as early as the Classical period, but were very unsophisticated, being made of clay, pottery or wood. Paper and plaster of paris were also used extensively in the making of toys.

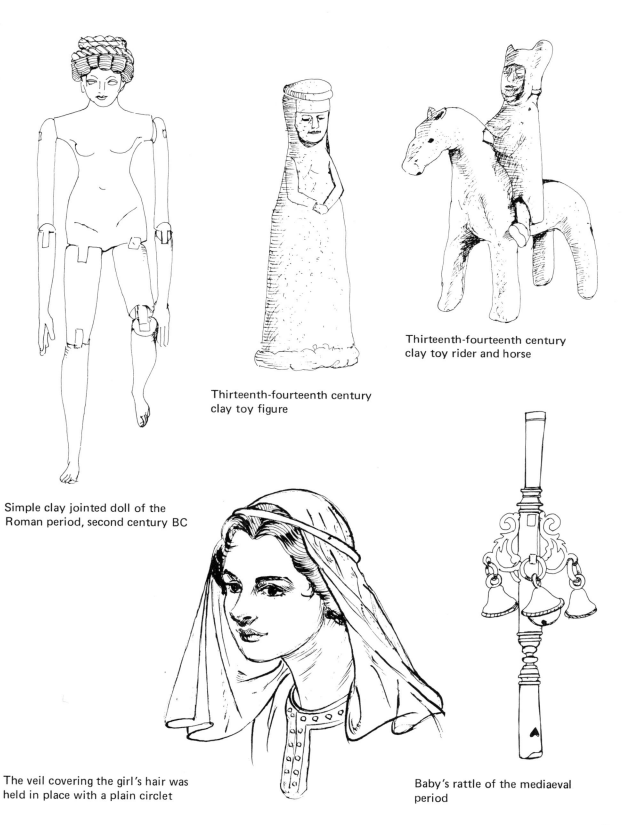

Simple clay jointed doll of the
Roman period, second century BC

Thirteenth-fourteenth century
clay toy figure

Thirteenth-fourteenth century
clay toy rider and horse

The veil covering the girl's hair was
held in place with a plain circlet

Baby's rattle of the mediaeval
period

Various headdresses and shoes of
the Roman period

The Early Britons

This young girl's dress, like an adult's, had a tight fitting bodice, the skirt falling in folds to the ground, with long tight sleeves that ended in streamers or tippets. The long hair is bound with ribbons, the ends encased in tubes, known as *foureaux*

The round stalked hat worn in the late thirteenth to early fourteenth century by young boys was worn over a linen coif which was tied under the chin. The loose over-tunic with an attached hood had deep armholes under cape-like sleeves gathered at the shoulders

Positive accuracy is not possible in the description of dress worn before the Norman period. Information is to be found only in religious manu-scripts and on murals. Primitive dress appears to have remained unchanged until the middle of the fourteenth century and was the same for both children and adults. Originally hide, and later cloth, was used to make simple tunics, capes and moccasins. Earth and vegetable colours were the first to be used as dyes.

If the material hung loose from the waist it was known as a *loincloth*; later to become a skirt. If the material was joined or passed between the legs, it developed into trousers which were more usual in cold weather.

Capes could be cut with a hole in the centre for the head to pass through or be semi-circular or rectangular.

In the Dark Ages the tunics were made of two pieces of skin roughly sewn together at the shoulders and down the sides leaving an opening for the arms.

Not before the second century AD were foot coverings made of pieces of skin tied to the foot.

The clothes were mainly adaptations of the fashions brought from other countries who had invaded Britain.

The Roman period

During this period Roman style tunics and semi-circular cloaks were popular. These were usually decorated with stripes, spots and even animal or bird designs. When the Romans left Britain around 450 AD, the Angles and Saxons were the new invaders bringing a new style of dress. The trend was for children to wear a straight, short-sleeved ankle length dress with a belted over-tunic having a slit at the sides to allow movement. Children often wore a hip belt from which were suspended small toys for the youn-ger ones, and real swords or daggers for the older boys of wealthy parents. Hair was generally worn long and loose although phrygian caps were popular. Trousers when worn were loose and cross gartered at the knees.

The Anglo-Saxon period

In Anglo-Saxon times the principal garment was a *gunna* which was an unbelted ankle length gown with the sleeves loose to the elbows. As embroidery was very popular, the neckline and sleeve edges as well as a panel down the front was so decorated. The designs were of Byzantine style. Under these full garments, long tight-sleeved gowns and chemises were worn.

Hair was worn rather long and veils were fashionable amongst older girls.

The Norman period

When the Normans came to power, shorter tunics with more jewellery became fashionable. A dramatic change was that boys' hair was now shaved close at the back. Tunics became shorter and closer fitting, with long fairly wide sleeves narrowing towards the wrists. A loose circular shaped over-garment was also worn, belted at the waist. Cloaks were semi-circular and fastened with clasps at the shoulders. These clasps and *fibulae* or pins were always popular.

Girls   Girls wore a gown or kirtle over a chemise which was usually longer than a boy's. Super-tunics were also worn. The cloaks were generally ground length and often had hoods attached. Their stockings were much better fitting than the *braes* worn by boys. Young girls wore their hair long and loose and covered it with a kerchief.

As no garments had pockets, belts and girdles were used to suspend small items.

Boys   Boys wore *braes* or breeches which were ankle length; tighter fitting for the wealthier classes. They were cross gartered or spirally bound with leather thongs. Shoes were flat without heels, pointed at the toes and close fitting.

Clothing consisted of a knee length tunic belted at the waist, the neck opening fastened with a clasp. Beneath this was worn a shirt. Hose were knee length and held up with garters or embroidered bands. Cross gartering was still popular until about 1066. Shoes became more ornate, fastening down the front with buckles, and were higher cut, like boots.

These children are dressed in typical early mediaeval clothing, some without any footwear. Their short gowns could have attached hoods. Very often, loose fitting sleeveless over-garments had a tie around the waist. Leg coverings could be made to fit, or be loose and cross bound up the legs. The flat-soled bootees seen on the foreground figure had thonging threaded through holes around the ankles to hold them on

Toys

The Normans probably introduced toy soldiers during the Crusades. Toy knights and horses made of wood or clay, were also very popular. Hobby horses were characteristic of the era and were of Anglo-Saxon origin. Spinning tops, whistles (made in the shape of birds) and little paper windmills (similar to those found in present-day fairgrounds) originated at about this time. Marbles were introduced to England from Belgium and Holland. Children were fond of ball games and skipping.

The Twelfth Century

Circa 1290   This toddler was dressed in a simple long dress with long sleeves

It was not until after the twelfth century that male and female clothing began to differ significantly. During the second half of the eleventh century the linings of women's outer garments were already of contrasting colours, and applique designs were used to a greater degree.

The Crusaders in the time of Richard I (1157-1199) brought back with them many Eastern ideas. The clothes became more generously cut with wider and fuller sleeves. Embroidery became more ornate and these trends lasted for many years.

The forerunner of the *cote-hardie*, which became popular in the fourteenth and fifteenth centuries, was a shaped and sleeveless gown with large slits from which the arms protruded. *Surcotes* or super-tunics were first introduced by the Crusaders and worn over other tunics, by both boys and girls. They could be of any length from the knees down, and were full. The sleeves could also vary in length. Openings were either at the sides or down the front.

Another style of outer dress, loose fitting from the shoulders, had very full long sleeves that were slit at the elbows so that the hands could protrude.

The poorer children had simpler clothes. They mainly wore loose tunics over shirts and drawers.

Girls

Tight fitting and clinging garments only remained fashionable until the end of the century when they became looser fitting, but still with the long hanging sleeves. Their cloaks were often fastened with cords so that the clothes beneath were revealed. The under-tunic was so cut that the skirt, which reached the ground, fell in voluminous folds and was seen beneath the over-tunic. Gowns closer fitting to the hips, became fashionable as did also more bell-shaped sleeves, or tight-fitting sleeves with embroidered cuffs. These became so exaggerated in the later part of the century that the ends had to be knotted. Girdles around the waist were richly embroidered and crossed at the back to be fastened in the front at hip level with the long pendant tassels.

Headwear and hairstyles   From the beginning of the century girls' hair no longer needed to be covered. It was worn in long plaits encased in silk. By the end of the century a net or *crespine* was being worn by young girls as well as by adults. *Barbettes* also became popular amongst the older girls. These were circular veils over the head, fastened under the chin. Sometimes they had a *chaplet* on the top. Bands of stiff material called *fillets* were worn around the head with either crespines or barbettes.

Boys
Towards the end of the twelfth century parti-coloured clothes became popular for boys. Tunics and hose were made in alternate contrasting colours.

Headwear and hairstyles   The Crusaders introduced shorter hairstyles. Boys' hair was cut short to the lobe of the ears and the front worn in a fringe. Headwear consisted of varieties of the phrygian cap until the late twelfth century.

Footwear and legwear   Towards the end of the century the loose braes became closer fitting and were tucked into the tops of the hose. Also popular were loose shorts with tunics or shirts tucked into the waist. When worn over the hose the tunics were long and heavily decorated.

Toys
Mediaeval toys were very simply made, mainly of clay and other natural materials.

Hoops, which became very popular, were originally made from the rings used around beer barrels.

Early twelfth century. The surcote or super-tunic with the rounded neckline was fastened with lacings at the back. These gowns with their large sleeves could be worn by boys and girls alike

The plain dress worn by this child had the common plain rounded neckline. The super-tunic or sideless surcote, like a tabbard, was worn over a kirtle and had a broad buckled belt over the hips. The hair was worn fairly long and loose. Shoes were becoming pointed and fastened around the ankles

10

The Thirteenth Century

Circa 1288 The overgown was longer and trained at the back, with the front shorter revealing the undergown. The little doll was also dressed in a simple gown

Towards the end of the century dress became very simple yet elegant. The long gowns were often unbelted, the outer ones so long at the back that they formed short trains.

Little girls were dressed in a type of surcote over which was worn a *bliaut*. This was a tunic that was only worn indoors. It was tight fitting to the waist and then allowed to fall loosely. It was generally sleeveless.

Headwear and hairstyles   Hair was worn long and loose with a plain circlet around the head. Coifs or bonnets were worn both indoors and out of doors. They were usually of linen. The habit of wearing a coif remained in vogue for centuries. Coifs were close fitting caps often worn beneath other headwear.

Babies

In mediaeval times babies were in swaddling clothes. This meant that their arms and legs were bandaged to the body from the neck to the feet, in the belief that this saved them from deformities or even their limbs from falling off.

By the time that they were about nine months old they began to wear simple long dresses with long sleeves.

Christening robes   These were also known as christening *palms* or *pales*, or *bearing cloths*. If the child died within a month, he or she was buried in this robe. These robes were often made of silk and richly embroidered; the shawl having an edging or fringing. The christening robes for the aristocracy usually consisted of long velvet fur-trimmed mantles with an extremely long silk kerchief reaching from the head of the baby down to the feet of the person who carried it.

Toys

Even from the thirteenth century the dolls were often jointed with string. (The German word *puppe* and the French *poupe* is an adaptation of the Latin *pupus* or *pupa* meaning baby.)

Bells attached to cradles, pull-along playthings as well as balls and hoops were already known to have existed as early as this.

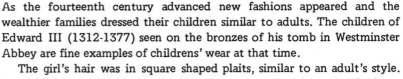

The Fourteenth Century

The high crowned fur hat of the mid fourteenth century was worn over a cowl decorated with dagging

As the fourteenth century advanced new fashions appeared and the wealthier families dressed their children similar to adults. The children of Edward III (1312-1377) seen on the bronzes of his tomb in Westminster Abbey are fine examples of childrens' wear at that time.

The girl's hair was in square shaped plaits, similar to an adult's style. Around the forehead was worn a band ornamented with jewels. The long, tight fitting gown was allowed to fall in folds at the feet. These gowns were generally plain without any ornamentation except for a front fastening with buttons and pockets at either side at hip level. Short sleeves had ground length streamers hanging from the upper part of the arms.

The boy's costume was also very plain and simple the with only ornametation being buttons down the front and a row of buttons from the wrist to the elbow. The tunic reached the top of the thighs and had a broad buckled belt over the hips. Both boys' and girls' dresses could have a low boat shaped neckline, giving them an elegant simplicity.

Girls

Little girls wore a *kirtle* as a kind of undergarment. This was a plain gown with loose sleeves that reached the ground but with an opening at the wrist for the hands to protrude. The gown was shaped to the body and embroidered around the hemline. It was closed with lacing from the neckline to the waist at the back. Children's necklines were not as low cut as those of their elders. The *cote-hardie* was worn over the kirtle. This was fairly close fitting with a low neckline which could easily be slipped over the head, so that it was not necessary to have a fastening. The sleeves generally ended just above the elbows, but had long narrow hanging extensions knowns as *tippets* or *streamers*. These could be dagged for decoration.

Outdoor wear Sideless surcotes, also worn over kirtles until the beginning of the sixteenth century, were low necked without sleeves, with large openings from the armholes at the sides to the hips. Often they were decorated down the front.

Headwear and hairstyles Coifs and veils were worn as headwear, although indoors girls often went bare-headed. Hair was dressed in similar styles to the boys, but could also be in roll curls above the ears.

Footwear and legwear Shoes were in the same styles as those worn by boys, being close fitting and laced.

The pointed cowl this boy is seen wearing was attached to a short cape. The loose belted tunic reached the top of the thighs over loose leg coverings. The shoes were tied at the ankles

Early fourteenth century. This boy is seen wearing a short cape with a liripipe attached. This example shows the liripipe hanging down the back. The tunic sleeves, tight fitting to the elbows, had plain wide extensions

Thigh-high hose were attached to a gipon or breeches with points or ties

Boys

Small boys wore loose fitting drawers secured with a running string around the waist. Over these they wore tunics which could reach the ankles, but which had a slit for easier movement. They could also be worn hitched up with a knightly girdle. Sleeves were usually loose and three-quarter length. Super-tunics, loose garments, were worn for ceremonial occasions and had long sleeves. The *gipon* replaced the tunic and was worn over a shirt. It was shaped slightly to the body and ended just above the knees or a little higher. The gipon was without a collar and had a round neckline, fastening down the front with either buttons or lacing. The long tight sleeves were buttoned from the wrist to elbow. Belts or girdles (often made of decorative metal discs) and buckles were worn at hip level.

Outdoor dress   Ankle length cloaks or mantles as well as thigh length capes were worn out of doors. These were often decorated with dagging or scalloping at the edges. Hooded cloaks and hoods were still popular but for ceremonial occasions boys wore jewelled chaplets on their heads.

Headwear and hairstyles   Hair was allowed to grow long, almost reaching the shoulders. All children wore hoods, generally lined in a bright colour. These had pointed cowls attached to shoulder capes. The cowls had prolonged points and were known as *liripipes*. Those worn by children were shorter than the ones worn by adults.

Footwear and legwear   Legwear consisted of hose. The close fit was achieved by cutting the material on the cross, and sometimes the soles were reinforced so that shoes were not essential. The hose reached the thighs and were attached to the gipon, and later the doublet, by means of strings joined to the underside of the gipon and threaded through eyelet holes in the hose. This method of fastening was known as 'trussing the points'.

Shoes, when worn, had ankle straps, and the uppers had punched-out designs. Towards the middle of the century they became more pointed and from about 1395 to 1410 piked shoes became fashionable. Shoes were fitted around the ankles and were laced on the inner side.

Accessories   Gloves were worn by many children and generally had gauntlet cuffs. They were made of leather or strong coarse material. Young wealthy boys from their early teens, or even before, carried swords as an ornamental accessory.

The dagged cowl with a short liripipe wrapped around the crown was buttoned together in the front

The Fifteenth Century

This girl is wearing a mediaeval truncated hennin headdress with a small frontlet

The little boy dressed as a page (*c* 1470) is wearing a gipon or doublet and hose. The doublets were well padded and ended just above the thighs. Attached to the waistbelt was a small dagger. The long tight sleeves of the chemise worn beneath the doublet protrude from the shorter ornamental puffed sleeves of the doublet. The soft buskins were laced down the inside edge of the legs

In the fifteenth century the gowns became loose fitting. Small girls' gowns were very similar to those of their mothers, but simpler. Even when very young their skirts were ground length.

During the reign of Edward IV (1442-1483) the boys of wealthy parents wore silk, satin or velvet doublets. The poorer classes wore them of linen or broadcloth.

Girls

Little girls were still dressed similarly to their mothers. They wore a chemise or smock beneath the kirtle or tunic which was close fitting with a low neckline and long tight sleeves. Fastening was with laces at the back. Over the kirtle, a sideless *surtout* or *supertunic* as it was also called, could be worn. This was popular from the middle of the century until the beginning of the sixteenth century and had a low neckline with wide armholes to the hips revealing the undergarments.

Dresses reaching just below the knees were decorated around the edges, often with scalloping. They almost always wore pinafores and these were slightly longer than the dresses.

Houppelandes   From about 1470 gowns or houppelandes were worn by both girls and boys. They were made with the top fitted to the body and allowed to hang loosely from the waist or hips. For the first time garments could be made with a seam around the waistline. The low neckline had a narrow falling collar that could be trimmed with fur to match the cuffed, tight fitting sleeves. A narrow belt could be worn loosely around the waist with long hanging ends. The gowns were generally closed with lacing down the front.

Headwear and hairstyles   Little girls' hair was often cut with a fringe in the front and curly at the sides. They wore coifs with small peaks in the front. Chaplets or wreaths of twisted silks as well as ornamented padded rolls were fashionable headwear. The hairstyle for older girls was to have very long hair in locks reaching to the waist. Like boys, girls did not wear any elaborate headwear, only simple veils.

Boys

Unlike men, small boys did not wear belts around their straight long gowns. These gowns had round necklines and were fastened by buttons

The girl is wearing a hennin covered with a veil and a frontlet on her forehead. Over the long under-garment, the over-garment was edged with fur

down the front or over the left shoulder. Sleeves were long, loose and straight.

When older boys wore gowns, these were only knee length. From about 1450 the necklines altered, a low stand collar becoming popular.

Doublets   Older boys dressed like men from the mid-century. They wore a doublet, previously known as a gipon, and hose. The doublet, padded and well fitting, was short, the skirts only just reaching the upper part of the thighs. This was fashionable until the end of the century. These waist length doublets had the sleeves and hose joined to them by points. Sleeves were generally close fitting, and the collars were of the stand variety from about 1450 to the end of the century, when a more square and lower neckline became popular. V-necked openings were also seen as well as the stand collar after 1450, the gap being filled with a stomacher over which the doublet could be laced or buttoned, or fastened with crudely made hooks and eyes.

Tabards were worn over the doublets with a belt around the front, allowing the back to hang freely. By the second half of the century the belt was raised from the hips to waist level.

Houppelandes   Over the doublet and hose could be worn a gown or houppelande. Unlike the long ceremonial gown of grown-ups, the childrens' version was about knee length and generally worn just for warmth. It was always lined and could be fur trimmed as well. When first fashionable, the houppelande had a close fitting neckline with a low stand collar, this was later rejected. The fullness of the gown concealed the button or hook and eye fastening that reached the hem. Waistbelts were always worn. The sleeves were long and full to a closed wrist, forming a hanging pouch that could be used as a pocket. This type of sleeve was peculiar to the houppelande, and was known as *bagpipe* or *pokys*.

Headwear and hairstyles   Young boys especially, were often seen without headwear. When worn it included caps, similar to coifs, bonnets with close fitting crowns and small turned up brims as well as hats of varying shapes. Hoods continued their popularity.

Hair became shorter than it had previously been in the fourteenth century and was curly or waved to the nape of the neck. Around 1460-1480 hair was worn with a centre parting, reasonably long, covering the ears.

Footwear and legwear   Hose, when they were not attached to the doublet, were joined at the crotch and went over the hips. Towards the end of the 1450s they reached the waist. A small pouch with a flap, called a *codpiece*, was fastened by ties in the front of the crotch. Separate hose were seldom worn except by the lower classes who wore them short and gartered at the knees.

The soled hose were still popular in inclement weather. *Pattens* were also worn with shoes and were extremely fashionable, especially in the period 1440-1460, when they were worn both indoors and out. These fashionable pattens had aspen-wood soles with raised cross bars at the heels and toes. They were buckled with a leather strap over the instep.

Childrens' shoes followed the fashions of the adults, being round toed for a while. They were generally made in one piece with a seam at the back.

Boots or *buskins* were also worn. These were fairly low to the ankles

and were closed with buckles and straps or they could be laced either down the fronts or at the sides. Shoes with ankle straps were only worn in the early part of the century.

From about 1460-1480 the piked shoes with their stuffed points again became popular amongst the older boys. These pointed shoes were known as *poulaines*.

Babies
In the fifteenth century babies were still in swaddling clothes. These *swathbondes* or *swathbands* were long strips of cloth in which infants were rolled, similar to the way Egyptian mummies were rolled.

Christening robes   The wealthier classes had sumptuous christening robes. The babies were wrapped in cloaks about 3.5 metres (4 yards) long, made of velvet and trimmed with miniver. Over this was placed, from the head and covering the velvet cloak, a long silk kerchief.

The boy with the long hair has a ► circlet around his head. The sleeve-less jacket, open at the sides, ends at the hips and is decorated at the edges and armholes with embroidery. The shirt sleeves are long and very wide. The hose with the soles attached to the feet are made to fit tightly

The close fitting doublet was buttoned to the high collar which revealed a small neck ruff. Over the armholes were padded wings with full shirt sleeves emerging ending tight at the wrists. The baggy hat with a narrow crown was decorated with feathers. Around his waist, as was not unusual, he wore a sword belt with sword. The voluminous trunk hose were paned with the bombast puffed out. The shoes were slashed for decoration

The little boy seen on the left is ► wearing a tabard which hangs loosley over his short gipon. The hose are tied to this with points. The small girl has a long loose gown or houpelande with a waistband and sham hanging sleeves over tight fitting long sleeves. This fashion followed very closely that of adults

16

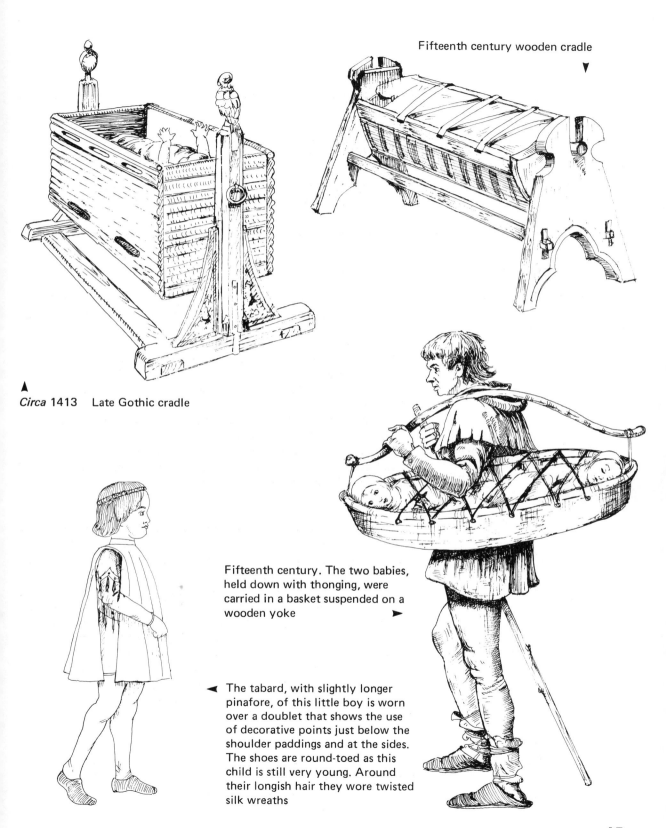

Fifteenth century wooden cradle ▼

▲
Circa 1413   Late Gothic cradle

Fifteenth century. The two babies,
held down with thonging, were
carried in a basket suspended on a
wooden yoke ▶

◀ The tabard, with slightly longer
pinafore, of this little boy is worn
over a doublet that shows the use
of decorative points just below the
shoulder paddings and at the sides.
The shoes are round-toed as this
child is still very young. Around
their longish hair they wore twisted
silk wreaths

17

The Sixteenth Century

The high-necked sleeveless jerkin was shaped and buttoned to the waist and a skirt was attached. Around his neck the child has a string of small toys, and a toy bird is seen in his hand

The ankle length gown had lunar shaped wings with long streamers attached which could be used as leading strings. The tight sleeves and neckline were decorated with ruffs, and the gown closed with buttoning to the waist. In his hand he holds a hobby horse on a stick

In the sixteenth century small children's clothes were of a practical design. They wore flannel gowns, bibs and biggins with plumed caps over them. These caps had turned-up fastened flaps. Boys and girls were dressed alike, at least up to the age of five for girls and eight for boys, and from then on boys were dressed more or less like their fathers, although they often wore slops or loose breeches.

Girls wore dresses that reached the ground, and when farthingales and ruffs became fashionable, they wore modified versions of these. Their headress was plainer than that of adults, mainly coifs or *billiments* being worn.

Materials used for children's clothing was of a cheaper quality, russet, a homespun type of hemp being used.

Guimps and ruched standing collars and even slashed sleeves were worn by children. Skirts and ruffs were starched for stiffness, and the toes of shoes became longer and more square shaped.

Girls

Ground length gowns were worn by small girls. These gowns could have the bodice and petticoat in different colours with the sleeves detachable, the shoulder join being hidden beneath the wings. The younger girls also wore aprons with or without bib fronts.

Ruffs, becoming fashionable in' the 1550s, were worn by girls when they reached their teens. The younger ones wore neck and wrist frills, or turned-down lace edged collars and cuffs. The older girls were dressed as adults, in gowns and kirtles, the kirtles from mid-century being just the under-skirt. The over-skirt of the gown was open in the front in an inverted V-shape, thus revealing an embroidered and ornate kirtle, also known as a *forepart* that often matched the sleeves.

Partlets were also popular with low décolleté bodices, the collars often of the standing style. Kerchiefs or neckerchiefs with lace or frills around the edge could also be worn to fill in a low décolletage.

Sleeves could be single or double. Small girls especially wore the simple loose but tight to the wrist sleeves. From about 1575 cannon or trunk sleeves, distended with padding or whalebone from the shoulders tapering to the wrist, were fashionable for the older girls.

Double sleeves were close fitting at the shoulders and widened towards the wrists to reveal the decorative under-sleeves which were often slashed, exposing the lining or sleeves beneath.

The bodice could have a high neckline, decorated with a circular ruff, or if the neckline was low, a fan shaped ruff could be worn. The bodice came to a point centre front, at the waist. Sometimes a stomacher was worn which was triangular in shape, the point ending just below the waist. They were very decorative. Waist girdles were sometimes worn and it was typical for a small book to be suspended from them.

For informal occasions and for warmth *nightgowns* were worn. These were loose and made unboned, but they could be very decorative and were often trimmed with fur. These nightgowns were not worn for bed as their name would suggest.

Farthingales From about 1545 when farthingales became fashionable, the kirtles were distended by several under-petticoats. Farthingales were petticoats supported by hoops made of whalebone, rushes and wood in a variety of shapes and styles. The wheel farthingale, an example of just one of the many varieties, supported the skirt horizontally out from the waist-line, tilting up slightly at the back. A gathered flounce was seen projected over the harsh line where the skirt fell vertically down from the wheel.

In the last years of the century the French farthingale, as well as a Spanish version, was worn. This was wheel shaped and had vertical sides. Petticoats were attached by tapes to the corset. The skirt was often tilted foward. The corset and bodice were laced at the back, and the front narrowed to a point giving a long silhouette. The sleeves were full and padded at the top. The horizontal part of the skirt was frilled radiating out over the vertical full skirt which reached the ankles allowing the feet to remain visible.

Outdoor dress For outdoor wear cloaks, cassocks and mantles were worn. The cloaks were generally three-quarter length, whilst the mantles were long, fastened with tasselled cords and worn on more formal occasions. Cassocks often had cape collars and were coats that were loose fitting with buttoning down the front. Circular cloaks made of a three-quarter circle, were buttoned down the front with the edges decorated either with lace in the summer or fur for the winter. They also had embroidered trimmings and were worn in various lengths.

At the start of the century draped hoods with embroidered lappets were fashionable. The draping of the hood hung at the back. From about 1520 stiff bonnets or French hoods were worn. These were placed further back on the head revealing the hair. The front edge was decorated with ruched or lace trimming or goldsmith's work, further ornamentation decorated the crown. These were known as *nether* or *upper billiments*. The draping or curtain at the back of the hood could be stiffened and could be turned up over the crown and worn as a peak to protect the face from sunburn. This was known as a *bongrace* and could be worn independently as a shade for the face.

Headwear and hairstyles Coifs were worn indoors by younger girls. Coifs or cauls were often made of silk thread with gold ornamentation and could be lined in coloured silk. Hair was allowed to hang loose and could be bound with hair laces or enclosed in a *chignon*.

Footwear and legwear Shoes were very similar to those worn by boys,

Circa 1585 The dress of this little child has a ruff around the neck. The long gown buttoned to the waist and has a girdle with a muckinder suspended from it

Circa 1540   This little girl is carrying a doll dressed in a similar style to herself. In the other hand is a toy cradle. They both wear Tudor style caps. Both the doll and the little girl have neck ruffs. The skirts of both are distended by several petticoats

Child's cap turned back revealing coif tied under the chin

the styles being of little consequence as they were generally hidden by the long skirts.

Slippers and mules, without quarters, were also worn.

Accessories   In the last quarter of the century light colours were popular. Little girls wore miniature versions of the usual Elizabethan fashions with petticoats showing beneath their skirts. Sometimes twisted scarves were worn to accentuate the pointed waistlines. Pockets were separate from the skirts, but could be reached through placket holes. The pockets were made of flat linen and worn tied around the waist. Amongst the items that they held were handkerchiefs which, for the older girls, replaced the *muckinder*.

Boys

Until they were six or seven years old, boys wore ankle length gowns with belts. Until about 1550 the necklines were low, showing the frilled shirt collars. The short sleeves with wrist frills were visible beneath the hanging sleeves which had winged shoulder pieces.

From the mid 1500s children of the wealthier classes, as soon as they were out of swaddling clothes, were dressed in clothes made of heavily embroidered and ornate materials. The gowns were to the ground and often with just wings. These were stiffened and decorated lunar shaped bands placed over the shoulder and arm seams. Pendant streamers were also attached to the back of the armhole openings and were useful as leading strings as soon as the toddlers began to walk.

Sleeveless gowns could have detachable sleeves, otherwise the shirt sleeves emerged trimmed with wrist ruffles that matched the ruffles around the neck that had replaced the earlier frills. Sleeved gowns, also with wrist ruffles, either had neck ruffles or falling bands. Most gowns were buttoned to the waist.

Until they were about eight many boys still continued to wear skirts, but by then they wore doublets rather than the female-style bodices. Carrying a sword for decoration was acceptable from this early age.

After the age when boys were breeched they were dressed in suits like adults. Doublets were worn over shirts, and in winter over padded waistcoats. They were always close fitting and waisted. At the beginning of the century they were without skirts, these gradually appearing, although at first they were not very deep. Doublets fastened down the front with either buttons, concealed hooks and eyes, lacing or points.

Until mid-century the neckline was low, but later a stand collar became popular. The sleeves could be detachable, fastening with points that could be hidden beneath wings. The sleeves could be close fitting or full to the elbow, but they were always tight fitting at the wrists.

Doublets and sleeves were sometimes quilted over padding. The doublets became shorter in the waist, but the overlapping skirts were longer in the early part of the century. Braid was used extensively to emphasise goring and slashing.

Boys in the late sixteenth century who were still at the age of wearing skirts nevertheless often wore small versions of peascod doublets with low necked lace collars. Very small children wore aprons over their clothes.

Jerkins or jackets could be worn over doublets buttoned or laced down

This very small boy is wearing a small cap with an ostrich feather decoration. The gown has a low boat-shaped neckline and is decorated with ruching. Streamers hang to the back from the elbow length sleeves. Necklaces were worn both by boys and girls

Circa 1538   Over the coif this little boy is seen wearing a flat cap decorated with a plume on top and aiguilettes sewn to the underside

the front. They were made similarly, unpadded but lined. They were generally without sleeves, or just had hanging sleeves. If sleeves were present they could be of the detachable kind. Sleeves were often puffed and full to the elbows, and then straight down to the wrists.

Overgarments, known as *gowns* (but not quite the same as those of infants) were worn over the doublets and jerkins, and were made very full with broad shoulders. They reached down to the knees and were shorter than those worn by adults. They were open in the front and were often edged with fur or ornate embroidery. Collars were often large and square and fell at the back, similar to a cape. The sleeves could be puffed at the top and hanging sleeves added as decoration. Sometimes they were just hanging sleeves with an opening at the top, allowing for the doublet or jerkin to emerge.

These gowns were worn for formal occasions (being black for funerals) more than the other styles of gowns known as *nightgowns* (nothing to do with night attire). They were worn informally mainly for warmth and by the older boys.

In the mid 1500s collars of gowns became narrower and higher, and the sleeves less full. Trunk hose were padded. Both jackets and hose had cut-out patterns through which puffs of material were visible.

Headwear and hairstyles   At the start of the sixteenth century it was fashionable for most young boys to wear skull caps; the more elaborate the cap the wealthier the parents. These caps were often of the same material as the gowns they wore. The more stylish caps were turned back at the front, exposing a bonnet-like coif tied beneath the chin.

About 1528 children's hair was often bobbed. The vogue was for slashed berets with a band of contrasting material held in place with a jewelled clasp.

Little boys also wore hats, small versions of their elders caps with baggy crowns and narrow brims, these were usually worn to one side and decorated with feathers. Over their coifs young boys could wear flat hats with a plume instead of the previous profusion of feathers. The under-surface could be decorated with *aiglettes*. Towards the middle of the century the pleated crown of hats became more raised, which later gave way to the hat band.

Caps, also known as *bonnets* with narrow turned-up brims and feather decorations were also worn. A typical style of flat cap was a flat mushroom shape over a narrow brim.

A flat cloth cap known as a 'City flat cap' (called a *statute* cap by William Shakespeare) was an essential part of costume. An edict made by the Statuary Court in 1571 was that all persons above the age of six, except noblemen and persons of degree had to wear flat beret-shaped hats on Sundays, and also had to show that they owned one. The reason for this decree was to safeguard the wool trade, encourage home manufacture and help employment, although this law was later repealed in 1597, being difficult to enforce as it was evaded and violated.

The Blue-Coat boys, the scholars of Christ's Hospital, wore them as part of their uniform with a long blue gown, buckled at the waist. These gowns were also the ordinary dress of people generally. Hats were usually made of felt or taffeta. Those of taffeta were known as *taffeta pipkins*

Circa 1548　The crown of the hat was pleated and decorated with a feather. The gown had a high and narrow collar, as did the jerkin with the low waistline and overlapping skirts. There was horizontal corded decoration with buttoning. The trunk hose and sleeves were padded and paned. The boy carried a small dagger

or just *pipkins*. These were fairly small, the round crown being pleated into a narrow brim. Decorated hatbands and feather trimmings were usual. The crowns of felt hats varied in height, but the brims were almost always narrow. Hatbands played an important part and displayed the wealth of the wearer. They were made of smooth material or of crepe and were decorated with jewels or embroidery.

Footwear and legwear　Until about 1540 hose were still worn by boys. They were similar to those of the previous century. The leg part was known as *nether stocks* and the hose were similar to tights, whilst the top parts were known as upper stocks until 1550 when that portion became known as *breeches*, being puffed out and padded down to the mid-thigh. The padding became known as *bombast*. *Paning* was also popular. These leg coverings were known as *trunk-*, *French-*, or *round-hose* as well as *trunk slops*.

In the reign of Edward VI (1537-1553) plain jerkins, doublets and hose were the general wear.

The codpiece in the hose, popular from the earliest part of the century, became less obvious after about 1570, and by the end of the century, was no longer seen.

From about 1568 knee breeches or Venetians were pear shaped, the very voluminous styles being known as *Venetian slops*. They were tied just below the knee level with garters (small sashes with a bow on the outer side).

The first knitted stockings were worn around this time. Until knitting became commonplace in the 1550s hose were made close fitting by cutting the material on the cross.

Knee breeches in the later part of the century, worn with garter hose became narrower with slits on the outer seams and were edged with buttons.

Stockings or hose were either knitted or made of material and tailored.

Ribbon or lace garters were tied above or below the knees. Boot hose or stockings were worn inside boots and made of a coarse material worn over more elegant stockings to protect them from dust and rubbing.

Shoes were generally close fitting to the ankles with square toes and flat heels, and slashings for decoration. Pumps for dancing with soft uppers were worn by children, usually made of Spanish leather.

Accessories　When dressed up for formal occasions the upper class of boys often carried swords and daggers as well as plumed hats. They wore baldricks, sashes and swordbelts.

Gloves were worn as well as mittens, the latter made with one division for the thumb and another for the fingers. Sometimes there was a horizontal slit in the palm to allow the fingers to emerge.

Babies

In the sixteenth century babies were wrapped in swaddling bands and wore biggins or caps on their heads, supposedly to help close the soft spot. The biggins were a kind of coif made of fine linen and were close fitting, fastening under the chin and covering the ears. Little boys occasionally also wore caps or high-crowned, narrow brimmed hats.

Shirts were often worn beneath the swaddling clothes, and occasionally

The skirted doublet, buttoned from neck to waist, had a small standing collar above which a small ruff was visible. The cape, reaching to the thighs was trimmed with fur. The trunk hose were paned and edged with braid revealing the padding. The codpiece was also seen. The flat bonnet or cap was pleated to a narrow brim and had feathered decoration. The tights were close fitting

▼

during the day they were allowed some freedom of movement, and were dressed in petticoats with little collars. They had short bibs and aprons with strings that were utilised to attach the muckinder and various toys as well as coral bars which were also useful during teething. At a few months of age babies wore long clothes with bibbed aprons and sometimes a girdle. Until they were at least one year old babies wore aprons and bibs. Muckinders were pinned to the waist or tied to a girdle. Bells, sticks of coral, both used for teething and lucky charms, were also tied to the girdle or pinned to the clothing.

In the Elizabethan era babies wore lace bonnets. Their coats were often decorated with embroidery.

Baby boys wore miniature versions of women's dress and when they became a little older they began to wear diminutive male clothes. Embroidered caps protected babies' heads, but children in general wore small versions of all types of adult headwear.

Toys
In the sixteenth century babies' toys consisted of balls and rattles, often made of ivory. These were hung around them on a belt over one shoulder, rather like a baldrick.

This boy wears a padded doublet, pointed in the front, just revealing the codpiece. The wings covering the cannon sleeve attachments at the shoulders consist of a double roll of padding. The short paned trunks show a lining of contrasting material. Many carried swords from their sword belts

▼

This is an example of an early ▶ sixteenth century schoolboy. The gown was long and loose with open sleeves. Attached to the girdle around the waist was a pen and ink horn. The hair was usually worn long and straight

Circa 1494   This baby's cap was close fitting with the ear-flaps tied up over the head. This was worn over a coif. Over the gown was worn a bib

Circa 1587   The baby is dressed in swathbondes with a hood pinned over the head. A pleated bib was pinned over the breast

This infant has a caul over which is worn a flat cap with feather decoration. The small neck ruff matches the wrist ruffs. The sleeves were full and decorated with jewels

Plate 1   Middle Ages. Performing Bears

The performing or dancing bear was a very popular spectacle of these early periods and drew an audience of children from different social classes. On the left is a boy from a wealthy family. The clothes are parti-coloured, the prevailing fashion of the time, both tunic and hose being made of different coloured materials, dividing the body into two parts. The sleeves are puffed at the shoulders. The short cote-hardie is sleeveless and drawn in by a belt at the waist, leaving the skirt neatly pleated in regular and precise folds. His short hairstyle is covered by a soft turban-shaped hat which falls over the brim. The long-toed shoes made of soft coloured leather are turned down from calf length to the ankles.

The small child, obviously of a lower class, is wearing clothes renovated or handed down. The plain gown was close fitting with long sleeves to the wrist. Over this was worn a tabard which covered the front and back of the body, but was open at the sides from the shoulders. A plain belt encircled the waist. No shoes was often the plight of the very poor. The girl, as with the poor at this time, wore the fashion of earlier periods. The costume consisted of three main garments the under tunic or gown which was hardly visible except for the long close-fitting sleeves, over this was an overgown, a close fitting garment with wide to the elbow sleeves, and for extra warmth a surcoat was worn over these, this sleeveless garment being slit at the sides down to the hips. The hair was concealed by a linen band that was wound around the head, fastened under the chin and further secured by a thin cord or ribbon around the forehead. The shoes, unlike the boy's, were not so exaggerated in length and fitted the foot, coming only to a slight point. The boy on the right, possibly middle class, wore a close fitting long sleeved under garment with hose. Over this he wore a short sleeved hip length cote-hardie which was drawn in at the waist by a leather belt. Over the head and shoulders he wore a *chaperon* with a *liripipe*. The shoes were the fashionable long toed variety with wooden pattens, the pointed ends supporting the shoes and attached with leather pieces.

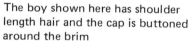
The boy shown here has shoulder
length hair and the cap is buttoned
around the brim

Mid sixteenth century wooden
cradle

Plate 2   Sixteenth century. Root-Ti-Toot, the Punch and Judy show

The sixteenth century was a period of mixed styles, when Swiss-German-English fashions
could be seen parading the streets. The Punch and Judy show was as much an attraction then
as it is today. The showman, dressed in the extravagent Swiss-German fashion with a hat with
a slashed brim of the early part of the century, banged a drum and blew the pan-pipes stuck in
his muffler. His dog, Toby, sat patiently with a ruff round his neck. The boy on the extreme
left is wearing a jerking type jacket with wide sleeves open from shoulder to wrist revealing
the short sleeves beneath. These wide sleeves are ornamented with buttons. The skirts of the
jerkin are quite narrow. The venetian breeches are full at the top, narrowing towards the knees
and fastened with a garter just below the knees. The stockings were usually made of yarn and
the footwear was close fitting. The older girl carries a doll dressed in clothes of the period.
She is dressed in a close fitting gown with a low waisted bodice, and long sleeves with wings
over the armholes. The gown, open in front, reveals a petticoat. The high neckline is surrounded by a linen collar. Suspended from the girdle is a pomander. The hair, parted in the centre
is covered by a French hood, the hanging piece at the back (the bongrace) could be brought
over the head and used as a protection from the sun.
The little girl in the foreground is wearing a close fitting gown with long straight lace-cuffed
sleeves and shoulder wings. Around the neck she has both a ruff and a collar. The short skirt
of the bodice is edged with scalloped lace. She also wears a narrow apron. A small skull cap
covers the back of her head.
The boy on the right, with his top and whip, is dressed in the fashionable 'peascod belly' or
padded doublet. The buttons shown down the front could be 'false', the doublet often being
fastened with hooks and eyes. The sleeves were in most cases detachable, the joins hidden by
the narrow stiffened welts or wings. The neck of the doublet is surrounded by a goffered ruff.
The short slashed trunk hose attached to the doublet by points or fastenings are concealed by
the short skirts of the doublet. The short hairstyle is covered by a narrow-brimmed soft hat
decorated with feathers. The shoes are close-fitting with rounded toes.

The Seventeenth Century

Circa 1690   The little boy is wearing a close fitting lace edged cap. He wears an apron over his dress with the virago sleeves

Children's dress reflected the fashion of their elders and although the extremes were not imitated, they were dressed in modified versions of adult styles. These fashions were simpler and less fussy although embroidery and lace trimming was still much in evidence for both sexes.

Miniaturised adult styles made children look like dwarfs, especially from the time of the Renaissance when wealthy people dressed their children in costly and elegant clothing as an outward sign of affluence. However in the confines of their homes the children took off their finery and generally wore just their undergarments — unbleached linen or woollen smocks and chemises. These were the only type of undergarment and were worn by men, women and children alike.

Right into the eighteenth century tiny boys and girls were clothed in ankle length dresses, the boys wearing them to the age of five or seven, after which age they were 'breeched'. Small boys wore doublets with stiff busk fronts whilst girls wore stiff stomachers in dark colours, often of greens and browns. Beneath these they wore hard corsets of *cuirbouilly* or boned canvas. The Stuart period saw the beginning of more natural and informal styles. From the early 1600s infants were in leading strings. These were made of a strong material and some were richly embroidered. Children in the mid-seventeenth century wore petticoats, stomachers, aprons and caps. Square toed shoes were the fashion. Hoops were worn beneath dresses, a fashion originated in Spain.

Long white lawn aprons, stiff bodices with straight white collars tied with tiny bows in the front, and matching sleeve cuffs were popular often worn over lawn stomachers. Close caps edged in lace were much favoured. Most of these garments were too long to walk around in and far too uncomfortable to play in as they were so stiff and many were lined with buckram. For everyday wear they were too ornamental and expensive. The linings were sewn with a coarse thread, although the needlework was generally most delicate.

Hanging sleeves were often used as pockets and were very popular.

Shoes and pumps were similar to those worn by boys, but girls' stockings were often of bright colours. They were held up with garters, tied either just above or below the knees.

Children wore soft leather kid slippers as well as shoes that were close and high with turned-down tongues and jewelled buckles. Towards the end

Circa 1650   The boy, aged about ten years wears a doublet buttoning to a high neckline that reveals a large turned down collar. The cloak bag breeches are decorated with ribbon loops. The tall sugar loaf hat has plumed decoration and ribbon bows. Hair was worn long and could be in ringlets

of the century children wore fringed gloves and carried miniature swords and sticks.

The development of embroidery was rapid in Elizabethan England and can be seen on almost all garments of that time.

Girls

Little girls wore long gowns and aprons, and about 1628 the gowns had slit sleeves. The aprons were often of silk with lace edging that matched the lace on their collars and cuffs, and were often embroidered around the edges. Velvet was a favourite material and the gowns were invariably decorated with ribbons and lace.

Long gowns similar to those worn by their mothers could have round turned-over collars with three-quarter length sleeves and turned back cuffs. From the shoulders hung narrow sham sleeves. Over the dresses children wore long pinafores of fine embroidered linen or muslin to keep their good expensive dresses clean.

The bodices of these gowns could be stiffened with whalebone, but sometimes little girls wore an under-bodice or stays that were stiffened.

The skirt part, known as a *petticoat*, was also sometimes referred to as a *coat*. These dresses or gowns were closed down the front with many buttons or ribbon bows. Until about 1620 when farthingales became unfashionable these, or stiffened under-petticoats, were worn to distend the skirts.

Waistcoats or jacket bodices without whalebone support or any stiffenings were worn for comfort and also sometimes at night to give extra warmth in winter.

Long sleeves were tight at the wrists. Cannon sleeves with vertical slashes like those worn by boys were common until about 1620, with wings fashionable up to about 1640. Virago sleeves, full and slashed, and tied at intervals, were also worn. Lace edged cuffs were common. Double sleeves similar to those of the previous century were worn in the 1630s, and the hanging sleeves after about 1630 became just thin strips of material forming sham narrow hanging sleeves that were ornamental when not used as leading strings. They were attached at the back of the armholes. These were popular for young girls until the mid eighteenth century. Until the 1640s ruffs were worn with high necked garments. These could be in a variety of styles — circular, falling or high at the back. Fan-shaped ruffs were only worn with low-necked décolletages. These were supported at the back with wire or *rabatoes*. Lace-edged falling collars or falling bands, as they were known, were fashionable from the 1650s when they started to become deeper. They were also called whisks.

Nightgowns, as previously, could be very ornate, but were made to fit loosely for comfort.

Outdoor wear   Cloaks were still popular, and soft hoods called *chaperones* were worn over coifs.

Headwear and hairstyles   Coifs or indoor caps were worn until girls reached their teens, usually lace edged or embroidered. Later they wore more grown-up styles of headwear, but also wore headscarves or cross cloths with the coifs. These were triangular in shape with the long straight border over the forehead, and the ends crossed under the chin and tied

The boy wears a close fitting doublet with a high standing collar and ruff. The cannon sleeves end with wrist ruffs. A ribbon belt holds a small dagger at his side. The codpiece is less visible than of previous times. The trunk hose were padded.

The young girl wears a close fitting bodice with a high standing collar also ending with a ruff that matches those at her wrists. From the short puffed sleeves are seen the tight under-sleeves of the under-gown. The overskirt is open at the front in an inverted V revealing the ornate under-garment

at the back.

In the 1640s children's hair was often worn in loose ringlets and fringes were popular. Close fitting coifs were still worn and might be edged in lace or braid. As decoration, plumes were sometimes attached. Little girls often wore their hair in the front combed back over a lace cap and pinned into loose curls falling down at the back. This style was similar to that of grown-ups.

Around 1660 large hats wirh ostrich plumes became the vogue. These hats were tied on with ribbons that often matched the ribbon band around the crown of the hat.

Towards the end of the century the *fontange*, a tall headdress with a close fittng crown, was usually worn on ceremonial occasions. The frills were supported by wires, and lace lappets often hung down the back.

Simple hairstyles remained fashionable. Hair was brushed straight back from the forehead, sometimes with a lock falling over the coif in front.

Accessories Aprons, buttoned up at the back were worn by girls of all ages, both as an ornamental accessory with lace edging and embroidery, and as a protection for the gown beneath. In the latter part of the century many boys as well as girls wore aprons known as *pinners*. These were pinned up bibs. They were also made in tiers and with sleeves that covered the whole garment worn beneath. Bibbed aprons without sleeves could also be worn. All girls in domestic service wore aprons.

Masks were used as a protection for the skin; half masks and loo masks were made of expensive materials and just hid the upper part of the face.

Horn books were carried with long handles which had a hole so that they could be strung round the neck. These books were made of wood and sheets of parchment and were covered with a thin layer of horn.

Boys

In the earlier part of the century little boys wore skirts that fastened with knots to the doublets, as did their breeches. Towards the end of the

28

Circa 1620   These two little girls are in dresses with full gathered skirts and aprons. The long sham hanging sleeves hang behind the sleeves with turned back lace cuffs. The fan shaped collar is made of lace and the low square decolletage is also lace edged. Even young children wore jewelled hair ornamentation. One of the little girls is seen holding a doll dressed in a similar fashion with a neck ruff and bibbed apron

Circa 1632   This little six year old boy is dressed in female fashions. He wears a falling band collar with matching cuffs. From the shoulders behind hang narrow sham hanging sleeves. The bodice is stiffened with whalebone, and ended in a point over the full skirt

century their coats were still cut rather straight, but were buttoned down the front. They had vertical slit pockets. The short outer sleeves with their narrow cuffs revealed the close sleeves of the waistcoats.

At the start of the century even very small children wore doublets and wide skirts. The doublets worn over the petticoats were buttoned down the front to the waist and a ribbon sash or belt was worn. The slashed or paned sleeves were fairly wide, and the hanging sleeves were relics of the leading strings used to control a child whilst learning to walk. Wings were usually present to cover the joins at the shoulder.

By about 1672 boys also wore blouses and jackets with their breeches, although the very little ones who were too young to wear breeches wore dresses similar to girls, but slightly shorter, and possibly not so tight fitting. Neck ruffs were popular until the 1630s, as were flat wired collars, after which date it was more usual to wear a white lace collar or falling band with matching cuffs.

When boys were breeched their outfits consisted of breeches and a doublet with square tabs, but by about 1670 doublets became unfashionable and were replaced by coat styles. In the first decade doublets were short with square tabs. After this time they became longer, until in the 1640s a looser, unwaisted style became the mode. Padding also became unfashionable after 1630, when just lining and stiff triangular fronts were sewn into them. These belly pieces became very fashionable. Sleeveless jerkins were worn over doublets only until about 1630. The coat styles which replaced the doublet from about 1670 were generally knee length with a slight shaping at the waist. They were without collars and lapels. The elbow length sleeves had enormous cuffs that were turned back, but towards the end of the century these became longer, reaching the wrists. Fastening was with buttons from the neck down to the hem line. Coats usually had a back vent and two side vents that ended with hip buttons,

Sleeved waistcoats without side vents were made in similar styles and were worn beneath coats. In winter under-waistcoats were worn as well for extra warmth.

Outdoor dress   Cloaks were of varying lengths and usually lined, often being made to match the doublet and breeches. They were mainly cut in circular shapes.

Headwear and hairstyles   Boys wore indoor caps until they were breeched. Hats were generally tall with flat crowns and large brims. Hatbands and feathers as well as ribbons were popular adornments. They were made of a variety of materials such as felt, stiffened silk or velvet, or beaver which was extremely fashionable. Towards the end of the century a three-cornered hat came into vogue.

Until the 1630s hair was worn short and brushed back to curl at the neck. As these styles became longer, centre partings were worn. From the 1640s they began to use hair powders, and gradually they also began to wear wigs.

Footwear and legwear   Breeches varied in style. From about 1568 Venetians or knee breeches remained popular. This was so until the 1620s from which time, and for about ten years, cloak-bag breeches were worn. These were fairly full, oval shaped, gathered at the knees and decorated with ornamental points or ribbon loops. Spanish hose then came into fashion. These were high waisted and reached below the knees and could be buttoned up at the sides with about ten buttons, or closed with ribbon bows. Sometimes they were allowed to fall loosely over the stockings. After about 1650 breeches were made to fit around the waist, so no longer needed to be attached to the doublets.

Stockings, usually of knitted material, were gartered below the knees. Stirrup hose or long stockings were first made without the foot. These were worn over silk stockings, serving the same purpose as the boot hose that had feet. The tops of these stockings were often lace edged and protruded over the boots when these were worn. *Gamashes* were high boots. These or leggings were worn as protection against the dirt. Both shoes and boots were round-toed until about 1635 when it became more fashionable for them to be square. Heels were gradually raised throughout this century.

Boots of soft leather were long and close-fitting and had bucket tops when worn for riding. Galoshes, or low overboots were often wooden soled and fastened with buckles. Until around 1680 shoes were open-sided with ankle straps and decorative bows or rosettes. Towards the end of the century they were more fashionable closed with high tongues and buckled or tied.

For dancing children wore soft leather pumps which were generally without heels.

Occupational dress   Linkboys or lamplighters were of the poorest classes and wore ragged clothes. In the late seventeenth century they could be seen in a shirt, ragged breeches, stockings and shoes, and an old tricorne hat worn on the side. They carried the tools of their trade which consisted of torches and oil cans, as well as scissors to trim the wicks.

Accessories   Gloves with gauntlets were worn. They were made of sheep-skin or soft leathers. Silk and woollen gloves were also seen, and perfumed gloves were worn by children of aristocracy.

Until about 1650 small boys carried rapiers, for swords and daggers were becoming less fashionable. Shoulder belts were gradually superceded by embroidered scarves worn diagonally from the right shoulder to the left hip from which to suspend weapons.

Hanging sleeves, fashionable in the Renaissance period and still popular in the seventeenth century were often slashed, but were now just an ornamental accessory. These sleeves were attached behind the functional ones and for children were longer than those of the grown-ups.

To make children's clothes more colourful the linings of capes and sleeves, for instance, as well as ribbon bows and tassels were red, yellow or other bright popular colours. Blue was worn mainly by the poorer classes.

Babies

In the early part of the seventeenth century swaddling clothes were still used. These often had a hard back, and were quilted and decorated with frills. Hands and feet were held in place with the bonding and the head was always encased in a cap or hood made of linen.

Infants' best clothes, not their everyday wear, consisted of christening

Circa 1618   The boy has short hair and in his hand is a plumed hat. Over his doublet he wears a sleeve-less jerkin with wings. He wears a crossbelt with a small sword attach-ed. The breeches are fairly full to the knees and the stockings well fitting. The shoes are decorated with bows

robes, fine skirts, petticoats and caps. Thin low-necked shirts remained a baby's underwear from the seventeenth century until the early 1830s. Thereafter silk and woollen underwear became more popular. This was usually edged in a narrow lace, corded or hem stitched, and embroidered with tiny designs. Linen shirts were worn by all infants from the time of James I (1603-1623). These tiny shirts had small revers or small collars made to turn over outside the robe like a small bib.

Babies who were too small to wear wigs, wore turbans. These were embellished with plumes and ribbons on festive occasions.

During the Commonwealth period (1649-1660) babies were dressed in linen clothes: a kind of bib for the top half with a piece of linen wound round the lower part of the body. On the head was a piece of material that fastened beneath the chin, and a shawl enveloped the whole body.

Swaddling clothes continued to be worn by all babies well into the eighteenth century, although dress clothes were worn for christenings and special occasions. They were usually of a pale yellow. These tiny dresses were invariably richly embroidered and the skirts about 100 cm (4 feet) in length. When babies were two or three months old the swaddling became less and under their dress they wore loose nappies which were easily changed when necessary.

Christening garments These consisted additionally of two figured or embroidered caps: the inner cap was tight-fitting, whilst the outer one was often turned back; and two palm or bearing cloths: the infant was wrapped in the smaller palm, over the petticoats, and placed on the larger palm. The person carrying the baby wore lace-trimmed cuffs and linen mittens trimmed with narrow lace.

Circa 1630 This child has shoulder length hair. A short cape covers the jerkin and crossbelt for the sword. The long legged breeches are tucked into boot hose

Toys

Balls and rattles were attached by long cords worn around the babies' necks. A bar was fixed to the front from which crosses and other pendants were hung. Belts and bracelets were also hung with playthings such as rattles, horns and teething rings.

By the end of the century the toy industry was a growing concern with an import/export trade. Simple toys gave way to scientific and clockwork models. Doll makers, originating in Germany, where the forests were a great source for the wood used, were craftsmen who made dolls with moveable limbs. These were to be seen from as early as the beginning of the fifteenth century. Wooden 'Dutch' dolls or 'Flanders babies' became popular in England, as were dolls' houses that were elaborately made with accurate reproductions of furniture and decorations of the period. These toys were also instructive as they were designed to teach little girls the art of housekeeping. Soldier dolls, popular with boys, were made of precious metals or lead for the wealthier classes, as well as of cardboard or wood for the poorer children. Miniature armies with guns and horses were encouraged as these aided military education as did drums and trumpets, also popular as they emulated military battles.

Wheeled rocking horses, although at first not well balanced, were popular as were Noah's Arks. Marbles and battledore and shuttlecock were among the favourite games of the period. Many toys were made with the affluent in mind, but cheap and simple toys remained a necessity.

Seventeenth century wooden cot frame

The Eighteenth Century

Late eighteenth century. This cape was cut in a semi-circular shape with a back vent, and fastened in the front with a bow

In the eighteenth century children were still dressed as miniature versions of their elders. Until the mid-century children, especially those of the upper classes, were dressed very formally. Boys generally wore silk stockings, breeches and lavishly embroidered coats. Girls were likewise dressed in similar clothes to adults and even had to suffer the tight boned corsets that were fashionable, as well as the hooped and heavily embroidered skirts.

Fashions remained basically the same from the 1680s until about 1715, although the male costume changed very little, even after that date, until the French Revolution in 1789 when there were dramatic changes. Then there was less ornamentation and embroidery, and female clothes became simpler, paniers and petticoats being discarded.

Eventually the reformation in dress, and the stiff, uncomfortable clothing gave way to more sensible dress suitable for children. In the very late part of the century a very short high-waisted style became fashionable and small pads or cushions were worn under the waistbands.

Both corsets and under-petticoats were discarded as the 'Classical' look became fashionable.

Children at this time were allowed to attend adult balls and were dressed accordingly.

In the late part of the century children's clothes gradually ceased to be just replicas of adult styles and tended towards more comfortable and practical wear.

About 1760 children wore stays to keep their posture straight. These stays were often of board, front and back, sewn to a buckram jacket.

Circa 1770   The pointed stiff bodice is decorated with a frilled front and the three-quarter length sleeves end in layers of lace. The overgown reveals the equally ornate petticoat

Circa 1700   The boy in the foreground is wearing a long collarless
coat buttoned from neck to hem,
with large round cuffs and flapped
pockets as the man. Both are
wearing tricorne hats. The man's
hair is powdered and held back
with a bow, whilst the boy's is

unpowdered in a similar style.
The shoes are with tongues and also
buckled. Stockings are held up
just below the knee with garters.
The boy in the foreground has a
hoop, a popular toy. The little girl
is wearing a flat crowned hat

decorated with ruching inside the
brim. The dress bodice comes down
to a deep peak in the front, like an
unstiffened crinoline dress. Covering the deep décolletage is a fichu.
From the wide cuffed short sleeves
are visible the fuller under-sleeves

Circa 1780   The skirt of the overgown was drawn up into a polonaise.
The tight sleeves ended in puffs
at the elbows. The bodice came
into a point in the front and had a
low décolletage. The hat, under
which a cap was worn, was tilted
forward with a ruching decoration

Circa 1702   The boy is wearing
a full bottomed wig and carrying a
tricorne hat. Both the jacket and
waistcoat were very ornate. Breeches
were knee length and the stockings
of silk

Up to 1775 boys wore boned but not basqued jackets like those of
little girls. As men's costume became more simplified so did that of the
children.

From about 1775 little boys' fashions included sailor suits with long
trousers, the jackets being short and loose. Waistcoats were also worn
at times with these outfits. In the last quarter of the century boys often
wore French type bonnets, lace edged, and held in place with a wide
band.

Towards the end of the century the children were permitted more
informal wear, the boys wearing open-necked shirts and plainer jackets and
trousers.

Girls
Small girls began to wear softer, unlined dresses in the later part of the
century. They were often made of muslin and were round necked with
either long or short sleeves. About 1715 the *sack* or *Watteau gown* with its
greater freedom and comfort became fashionable. This was shapeless with
a full and loose back, but by the mid 1730s open gowns with hoops were
in vogue. Paniers and very full skirted dresses followed, although bodices
thoughout the period had a slim long-waisted appearance.

Simpler dresses appeared in the mid 1700s, a fashion followed by adults
towards the 1780s. These dresses were less boned and more chemise-
shaped, worn with a sash around the waist.

Up to about 1775 little girls wore sheath dresses and fichus, although
stiff bodices and panier skirts were still being worn. Gradually the rigid
bodices and powdered wigs went out of fashion, linen frocks with sashes
becoming more popular. Muslin sheath dresses over taffeta under-skirts
with a sash were also the mode. Dresses were printed or embroidered in
all kinds of motifs and could be flowered to match the hair decoration.

Décolletage was oval or round and generally edged with lace or net. The
elbow length sleeves ended with puffs frilled to match the neckline.

Miniature hoops or petticoats were worn beneath the dresses. Aprons
were always worn, and often embroidered at the hem.

Girls were allowed to shed their tight corsets and heavy hooped skirts
and wear simple dresses that could be gathered at the waist with ribbon
bands.

In the last quarter of the century simple muslins revolutionised children's dress.

From the 1770s the ground length dresses became shorter to above the
ankles revealing the more comfortable slippers made of kid or fabric.
Heavier buckled shoes became less popular for wear with the daintier
dresses. Girls who until about 1778 were dressed in the restricting clothes
of their elders were now clothed in lighter fashions made of muslin and
printed cottons with the skirts just reaching the ankles. Wide sashes were
worn fairly high above the natural waistline.

About 1780 the bustle-style look, so popular in the 1680s, became
fashionable again. It was often known as the *polonaise*.

Cloaks of all lengths were popular at this period.
Headwear and hairstyles   Girls' hair was dressed in similar fashion to the
ladies'. This was achieved with the use of curl papers, irons and pomade.

Circa 1802   The little girl is wearing a simple high waisted dress with a square neckline and short sleeves. She is holding up the long train. The little boy is wearing a plain suit, the top has a large rise and fall collar and is short to just above the waist. The trousers are high above the waist, but end just above the ankles

Circa 1745   The little girl wears a long mantle with hood and collar attached buttoning down the front. There are slits for the arms to protrude

Little girls in the time of Queen Anne (1702-1714) wore large full-bottomed wigs even before they reached the age of seven. During the time when wigs were in vogue, boys' hair was dusted with powder and was dressed in a similar manner to the wigs. Until about 1780 both boys' and girls' hair was worn curled and powdered.

Around 1745-1750 girls' hair was worn with ringlets and the front of the hair was pulled over a pad and could be decorated with artificial flowers. Towards the end of the century small pinners, or caps which often had white streamers trailing at the back, were fashionable. Straw hats were popular in the country, and both boys and girls alike wore them. They often had a ribbon band around the crown with a rosette for decoration.

The *pinners* or mob caps in the later part of the century were trimmed with ribbon bows and made of a flat circular piece of material or broderie anglaise, with a tape around the brim to draw them together. This facilitated washing and ironing. They were usually starched to give a firm shape. The edges could be frilled and the front decorated with a large ribbon bow.

School dress   Towards the end of the 1700s Charity School girls wore small pleated caps upon stiff upturned hair. Their dress consisted of a bodice and a stomacher with long tight sleeves, the open gown being held off the ground, often worn drawn through the pocket holes. Long mittens were worn as well as long white aprons. This period costume was retained in many parish schools, at least until the middle of the nineteenth century.

Boys

In the mid-century boys who had not yet been breeched wore a compromise between male and female fashions. They wore male wigs, coats that had cuffs and buttoning like the mens' and had low décolletages of female attire. A sash could also be worn around the waist.

By the mid 1700s dress materials became plainer and there was less embroidery to be seen. Coat cuffs became smaller.

Fashionable from the 1790s to the mid-nineteenth century were suits known as *skeleton* suits. The jackets were tight fitting with rows of ornamental buttons down the front. The ankle length trousers were buttoned to and over the jacket just above the waist, under the arms. They had either fall fronts or fly-front fastenings.

By mid-century a five year old boy might be seen wearing a frock with petticoats to the ground, and a tight fitting waistcoat with silver buttons and lace trimming. The coat could have broad cuffs, wrist ruffles, frogging and turned-over revers. Another type of coat fashionable in the same period opened in the front to reveal a satin petticoat. Some coats had a low neckline with elbow length sleeves that revealed full under-sleeves.

Headwear and hairstyles   In the mid century boys between the ages of ten and twelve wore tricorne hats similar to their elders. Their hair however was their own and was worn unpowdered in general. It was long and curled with ribbon bow ties to hold the *queue* at the back.

Eighteenth century students wore the fashionable tie wigs with the hair drawn back and tied with a black ribbon, allowing the curls to hang down and form a queue. From the early part of the seventeenth century students

Circa 1775 The girl has a large mob cap with lace edging. Her hair falls down loosely at the back. The short jacket has elbow length sleeves and deep round cuffs and ruffles. The lace on the neckerchief matches that surrounding the jacket. The stomacher ends in a V shape and the skirt is long and plain

Circa 1790 Mob cap showing the soft hairstyle. The dress is in a simple muslin with a wide ribbon sash

wore a type of mortar board.

Footwear and Legwear Shoes were seldom seen in contemporary paintings, but boys wore black square-toed ones with buckles, whilst girls wore slipper type shoes with the toes turned up and ornamented from the instep down to the toes. These resembled Turkish styles.

Shoes were generally black, or at least very dark, but they had red heels. They also had tongues and metal buckles throughout the century.

Occupational dress Stable-boys and undergrooms wore loose jackets, usually in brown in the late 1700s. They also wore waist length coats and brightly coloured waistcoats. Cravats were also fashionable. For legwear, breeches and leggings with top boots were usual.

Chimney-sweeps were usually small boys who had to climb up the chimneys to scrape the soot away. They were dressed in clothes of the period but inevitably soot-stained. The usual apparel in the eighteenth century was a jacket with a belt, breeches, shoes and stockings, and a soft cap. The caps very often bore a badge showing the name and address of the boys' employer.

Babies

Babies were no longer encased in tight swaddling clothes, and the older children were even permitted to be bare-headed. The habit of swaddling had gradually died out. However, a relic of the swaddling bands was a *binde* or slip which was a straight piece of material with vertical tucks to shape it to the body and wound around it. Tiny linen shirts were also worn. These had round or slightly square necklines, were open in the front and generally made of one piece of material sewn together at the shoulders with gussets beneath the arms. The sleeves could be slightly gathered at the shoulders and reached the elbows. Both the sleeves and the neck opening could be lace edged or frilled.

Dresses, when worn, were generally round or square necked and revealed the shirt neck. Shirts were worn beneath flannel petticoats and linen or muslin slips were worn over the petticoats. The shirt sleeves also peeped out over the dress sleeves that could have turned back cuffs. The dress bodices might be stiffened with quilting or a stiff material. Back openings were common, and the full skirts reached just below the feet, right until the infant began walking, when of necessity the skirts became shorter. Waist sashes were placed higher in the second half of the century, when necklines became lower. All babies wore caps night and day from the time that they were born. During the latter part of the century the caps were embroidered or lace edged. Boy infants wore a holland cap with cambric borders and their sleeved gowns were often of dimity.

Christening robes Christening robes were usually made of a white satin and were very long. They opened down the front with the bodice shaped with the aid of tucks. Sleeves were often detachable. Silk braid and knotted fringes were a popular trimming. Long ornamentally laced bibs were worn. Caps and undercaps as well as overmantles were also seen. At first they wore two caps, a plain undercap and a frilled or lace one over. These could take the form of a triangular piece of material with lace at the front edge and tied, passing beneath the chin and fastening on the head. The caps were generally made in pieces, a central ornamental piece and two

Circa 1690   The young girl has a fontage headdress made of lace and ribbon bows with the lappets hanging down at the back. The hair was worn up with just a few curls on the forehead and a small face patch covered blemishes

side parts. The caps were often quilted or made of stiff material and embroidered.

Toys

As the printed word became more readily available children were able to have their own books. Paper or card were also popular for making all kinds of toys. Pictures were printed of dolls and dolls' furniture as well as ships, soldiers, etc, stuck on card and then cut out. In this way dolls could be dressed in various styles, as the clothes could be made separately and attached with tabs to the dolls.

Dolls' houses were first designed by architects, and the furniture fashioned by apprentice carpenters, famous names such as Chippendale being among them, although many were also home made. Dolls in the eighteenth century were still rather stilted. Many were very basic, made of wood with leather arms and hands, and painted heads. Wooden shafts were put through the shoulders to attach the arms, making them mobile, the same principle was later applied to the elbows, hips, knees and ankles. Glass eyes were also used, although eyes were mainly painted on at this time. The dresses of the dolls always followed the fashions of the day. Automated and mechanical toys became extremely popular in the eighteenth century. Clockwork mechanisms were used in a great variety of toys, for movement as well as for music and speech. They were used in birds, animals, musical boxes, dolls, and so forth.

Circa 1780   The boy is seen wearing a frock coat and breeches. The shoes were buckled. As can be seen there was less ornamentation in the later part of the eighteenth century ►

Circa 1770   The boy wears his hair curled with a queue fastened behind with a ribbon bow tie. The tricorne hat was also popular

Circa 1799 The gentleman between the two children is wearing a jacket, tight breeches and stockings. The boy is dressed with a shorter, similar jacket and long tight trousers. The large shirt collar edged with frilling lies over the waistcoat and jacket collar. The little girl has a bonnet framing her face and is wearing a cape with a large collar attached over a simple loose dress

▼

Circa 1740 This carved and painted wooden doll was dressed in period clothes

The Nineteenth Century

Circa 1861   This little two-year old boy dressed like a girl with masses of petticoats, shows the wide drawers beneath

Circa 1830   The earlier tighter sleeves were replaced by short puffed ones. The sash was above the natural waistline and the pantalettes were ankle length. The soft shoes had cross ribbon fastening

In the early nineteenth century children's clothes were made of light washable materials, the styles differing only slightly from the grown-up modes. Both small boys and girls wore ankle length pantelettes. Whilst the simple clothes of the Empire line were fashionable, children's dress followed this mode, but when they again became more elaborate children's wear followed more slowly.

In the mid 1800s little boys and girls wore waist crinolines. Little boys also still wore sailor suits although these had in fact no resemblance to an actual sailor's outfit. The fashion for sailor styles lasted for well over one hundred years, although it varied as the fashionable silhouette altered.

In the 1860s children's clothes were mentioned in fashion magazines for the first time. When advertised or shown in these magazines it was always stated the age for which a particular item of clothing was designed. Tailors even designed clothes specifically for boys up to the age of five, who were still in dresses. Pleated skirts were attached to bodices and were very popular. After the age of five, until they were about seven or eight, boys began to wear jackets and breeches that buttoned at the knees. Thereafter well cut jackets and Louis XV breeches were worn.

Girls

Girls were dressed in adult fashions apart from a few variations as soon as they were out of their infancy. In the first part of the century they wore long skirts, short sleeves and low necklines. In the second half, skirts became shorter, and apart from party dresses, higher necklines and long sleeves became the mode.

Pinafores and aprons were worn to keep the dresses clean. In the later years of the period smocking on the yokes of dresses, waist and sleeves became very popular.

One of the most attractive styles of children's wear was seen early in the nineteenth century. This was a high waisted Empire line, as popular with women as it was with small boys and girls. Playclothes or clothes worn for everyday were often made of muslin or nankeen.

Little girls wore slips beneath the full unlined lawn and muslin dresses, these had sashes just above the waistline and were made in simple styles. From about 1825 girls were again dressed in similar styles to grown-ups, with aprons that were edged with ruching. From the 1830s the waistline

Circa 1810　This little girl wears a high waisted Empire line dress with lace edged drawers protruding

Circa 1887　The little girl is wearing a pinafore over her dress. Her shoes are fastened with a button and strap

was lowered to its normal place and the skirts once again became fuller. Sleeves also altered in shape. They were in the leg-o'-mutton or puffed styles. A great deal of ornamentation became popular, dresses were profusely decorated with ruffles, ruching and ribbon bows as well as an enormous amount of embroidery. Lighter materials such as organdies in richer colours were also used.

In the 1860s girls also wore skirts, and blouses that were in the style of men's shirts. These were originally mainly worn for sports and were fashionable for girls before the adults actually adopted the style.

Even very young girls wore full length stiffened corsets when the waist level which had been high at the end of the eighteenth century, came to its natural level from the late 1820s. The corsets were pulled in extremely tightly at the waist to emphasise the smallness, thus enhancing the full skirts that had anything up to ten wide stiffened petticoats beneath.

The sensible dresses of the early 1800s gave place to more elaborate dresses in the 1850s with the frilled pantalettes again coming into vogue, peeping beneath the skirt hems.

Dresses had horizontal flounces and raised embroidery. Fringed sashes were also popular.

A girl's age could be judged by the length of her skirt; just below the knees to the age of twelve, then calf length until fourteen, and at sixteen, down to the ankles. From the age of seventeen or eighteen the skirts were ground length, just as the grown-ups'.

Basqued bodices with long waists were popular in the 1870s and 1880s. From about 1880 little girls no longer wore miniature versions of adult clothes, but were fashionably dressed in straight dresses over fully pleated false skirts with a wide belt at almost knee level, just a few centimeters above the hem of the skirt. This style with variations remained popular until the end of the century. Sometimes the bodice was slightly bloused and was belted at the waist. Whilst the bustle was fashionable amongst the grown-ups in the period between 1883 and 1886, little girls also wore less exaggerated forms of the polonaise style.

Scottish modes and Russian styles in blouses were periodically popular, but the sailor suit fashion remained in vogue the longest, this fashion beng worn by both boys and girls.

Crinolines　Young girls were dressed in replicas of adult attire and even the youngest had to wear the universal crinolines. From the 1840s crinolines were the mode. The earlier ones were very full starched petticoats worn over one of flannel, or else they were stiffened with crin (horsehair). By the 1850s the petticoats were made of wire hoops taped together and known as the American cage, and they were much lighter in weight.

From the 1850s when the lighter crinolines had been invented, little girls were delighted, as it liberated them from the weighty and cumbersome layers of petticoats. Under the crinolines they wore long linen pantaloons that could reach the ankles and were edged with tiers of lace. Those whose parents could not afford to buy the full pantaloons wore pantalettes which were just tubes of frilled linen, ending just above the knees. Long frilled drawers also sufficed.

In the 1860s the fullness of the skirts was beginning to be pushed towards the back, and by the 1870s the bustle had come into being.

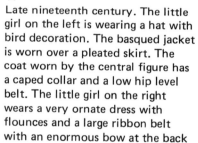

Circa 1857   The apron is edged with ruching. The fullness of the skirt is pushed to the back giving a bustle effect. The hat is of hard felt with a turned-up brim and feather decoration

Circa 1860   This quite plain dress was pushed out from the waist with petticoats, the lace of which was just visible

Late nineteenth century. The little girl on the left is wearing a hat with bird decoration. The basqued jacket is worn over a pleated skirt. The coat worn by the central figure has a caped collar and a low hip level belt. The little girl on the right wears a very ornate dress with flounces and a large ribbon belt with an enormous bow at the back

Circa 1850   The dress was heavily flounced and from the shorter flounced sleeves could be seen longer full sleeves. The lace edged pantaloons could be seen beyond the hemline

Circa 1885   The hair is worn long and loose. The coat is pushed towards the back, giving a slight bustle effect. The high boots were made in two tones

Circa 1830   The full skirt shows both the petticoats and frilled drawers. The tight fitting bodice has a low wide neckline. The ever popular hoop and stick is held in the hands

Circa 1860   This little six year old girl with her hair held in place with a ribbon is in a party dress with short puffed sleeves. Her drawers show from beneath the hemline

Circa 1835   The girl is dressed in typically mid-Victorian style. The bonnet frames her face and is tied down with a bow beneath the chin. Her hair has the fashionable centre parting. From beneath the flounced skirt are seen the pantalettes that hide the ankles

Circa 1816   An Empire line dress with frilled pantalettes showing beneath. The base of the dress is profusely decorated with frills

Circa 1850   The fashionable bonnet is tied under the chin with a ribbon bow. The jacket is decorated with frogging. The tartan skirt beneath is worn over a light crinoline and the drawers peep from beneath. The boots are ankle high

Circa 1841   The little girl has her hair in ringlets and is wearing a bonnet with the strings untied

Circa 1872 The party dress is trimmed with broderie anglaise and has a wide sash with a bow at the back. The long hair has a ribbon tied in a bow at the top. Half boots are worn over short socks

Although children's wear still resembled the adult styles, they were less cumbersome, although still impractical.

Pantalettes Clothing again became more cumbersome with long ankle length pantalettes which were trimmed with lace, and wide skirts that were decorated with ribbons. In the early nineteenth century the pantalettes peeped from below the high waisted skirts. Ladies did not begin to wear drawers until 1806. At first, frilled false pantalettes were worn at the knees to hide the legs, but later drawers or pantalettes were fashionable and were visible beneath the shorter skirts. Gradually they became narrower and declined in popularity. Cambric ankle length drawers were worn; the lace edge peeping below the skirts was especially fashionable until the 1830s when these became shorter. The drawers often had attachments buttoned to them, either for lengthening or to keep them clean.

Pantalettes, when worn, also became shorter, and like most white clothing, were covered in a profusion of embroidery, notched edges and eyelets, in the Victorian era.

Sailor dress The basic sailor outfits had square collars with white braid edging which came to a point over the striped front. The trousers for boys could be either long or short in a blue or white serge. Even striped materials could be worn. Little girls wore pleated skirts in the same colours. Before the twentieth century, instead of a blouse, a 'quartermaster jacket' was often worn over a striped front or plastron. A sailor beret completed the outfit for both boys and girls.

Headwear and hairstyles Headwear was always worn out of doors. Popular were sailor hats, similar to those worn by boys. Until the 1830s white caps were sometimes worn beneath bonnets. Even for play outdoors headwear was a necessity.

In this century most little girls, like their grown-up counterparts, wore bonnets which were held in place under the chin with ribbons. They were made of various materials including straw. They could also be made of lace or linen and clusters of artificial flowers or ribbon bows were sometimes used as adornment.

In the mid-nineteenth century girls wore flat straw hats with ribbons. In the latter part of the century they often wore broderie anglaise hats gathered with tape which could be untied for easier laundering. Very often another hat, perhaps of silk could be worn over this.

Large bows were very fashionable and were seen on many young girls' hats and they were also popular with teenagers.

For school wear tartan tam-o'-shanters were popular. These usually had a pom-pon on top. Only in private schools was the wearing of hats compulsory, and these only from the end of the century. The hatbands always bore the badge of the particular school. These school hats remained in vogue until the mid-1950s when hats in general became less popular.

Hair was allowed to grow quite long and hang down in ringlets tied together with bows. Side partings were fashionable. Ringlets were made by twisting the hair in rags or curling papers overnight. When the girls reached the age of seventeen when they were regarded as grown-up, they began to wear their hair on top of their heads, the fashion of the day.

Towards the end of the century children's hair was long and combed in loose curls. Often they had large bows on top of the head to keep the

Circa 1840 This little girl has her hair in plaits hanging either side

Circa 1855   The hair is worn smooth, parted in the centre and the ornamented hat has streamers behind. The dress is very flounced and beneath can be seen the pantalettes. Ankle length elastic sided boots were also worn

Circa 1856   This little girl's bonnet is tied under the chin with a huge bow and the full skirted party dress has a wide ribbon sash around the waist

Circa 1896   This dress is smocked at the yoke and falls loosely. The sleeves are the big leg-o' mutton style with epaulettes

Circa 1896   Under her ornate headwear the little girl has her hair in long ringlets. The coat has large leg-o'-mutton sleeves

Various hairstyles of the nineteenth century: (a) *c* 1874 (b) *c* 1892 (c) *c* 1880 (d) *c* 1874

44

Circa 1881   Hat with feather ornamentation

Circa 1886   Toque style hat with ribbon and pom-pon decoration

Circa 1894   The boy, carrying a hockey stick, wears a school cap with a badge, a long polo necked jumper and knickerbockers

Circa 1860   The hair is parted in the centre with the hair plaited either side. The day cap has streamers

Circa 1892   Little girl in a broderie anglaise hat with a soft silk over-hat

Circa 1893   The little boy is dressed in a reefer style jacket which has a large lace collar and matching cuffs. The ankle-length skirt is in large pleats and the high shoes were buttoned to above the ankles

Circa 1820   The little boy is wearing a skeleton suit with high trousers that had a fall front. They are buttoned to the top which is decorated with two vertical rows of buttons. The ever-popular hoop with stick can be seen in his hands

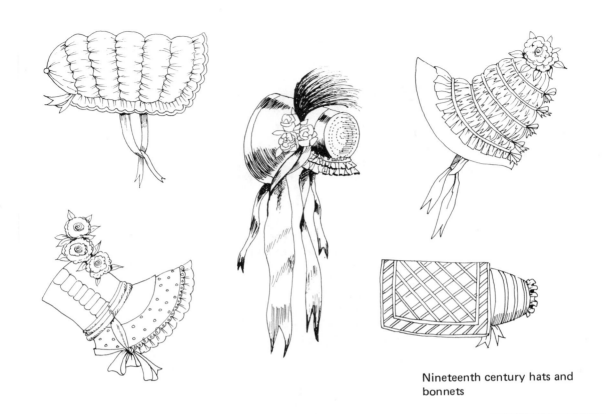

Nineteenth century hats and bonnets

Circa 1857   This boy is in the transition of being dressed in an adult type suit. The jacket is more casual and has a bow at the collar, being open without fastenings to reveal the waistcoat beneath

Circa 1810   This skeleton suit would only be worn after the age of four. The frilled shirt collar was worn over the suit collar. The sleeves from which protruded the shirt sleeves were excessively long as was the mode

◄ Hats and bonnets of the nineteenth century: (a) cap with peak and loop and button decoration *c* 1854 (b) cap with a tartan band and tassels *c* 1854 (c) bonnet with lappets *c* 1868 (d) hat with a profusion of pleated materials *c* 1896 (e) tall crowned bonnet (f) bonnet

hair away from the face.

When long hair was in vogue, those children with straight hair had it brushed smoothly and held in a snood. Centre partings, like Queen Victoria's, were fashionable for some time. Occasionally girls were seen with their hair cut short, like that of the boys.

Footwear and legwear   Towards the middle of the century buttoned shoes with pleated cuffs around the ankles, and boots were all styles worn by girls. Striped stockings and coloured shoes were fashionable, as were gaiters in the 1850s. Brown and black buttoned shoes were worn with long white stockings in the 1870s, whilst in the 1880s black or brown shoes were worn with stockings of the same colour.

Accessories   Handstitching and embroidery as well as lace was always popular on small children's clothing.

Aprons and pinafores remained a part of girls' wear at home and school to protect their dresses. For parties and special occasions aprons were made of very fine material or of lace, and richly embroidered, being worn as a decorative accessory.

Boys

Until the age of four or five small boys still wore skirts, later wearing long trousers when they were breeched. They also wore bowler hats and those made of straw when they became fashionable later in the century.

In the early part of the century (1815-1840) boys up to the age of five were still dressed in the same style of clothes as girls, after which age they wore long trousers or pantaloons. Long tunics, some reaching the knees, were worn over trousers with shirts beneath that had wide collars appearing over the tunic neckline.

When boys reached the age of twelve, trousers with short jackets were more the vogue. Only when they reached their teens were boys dressed completely in adult fashions.

During the Romantic period, in the 1830s, children wore trousers, pantaloons or pantalettes that were frilled at the ankles showing beneath the skirts. In the beginning of the 1840s the edges of outer garments were trimmed more and more with corded patterns which later in the 1850s developed into ornamental braiding and fringes.

In the Victorian period tartan became very fashionable and small boys were clad in Scottish dress and Glengarry bonnets.

In the mid 1800s boys still wore skirts over trousers and dresses and tabbed jackets were still popular in the 1860s.

Tunic suits were also worn by young boys in the 1840s and 1870s. The tunic was actually a jacket close fitting to the waist, and the skirts which reached the knees were pleated to the bodice part with a belt around the waist. These were often worn with trousers. In the 1850s boys up to the age of about six wore tunics, but without long trousers, drawers showing from beneath. Under dresses they were able to wear either trousers, or more usually, pantalettes.

The knee-length tunics were belted at the waist. Their sleeves were as varied as those of the girls and could even be of the leg-o'-mutton style.

In the 1860s crinolines with tight fitting bodices were still worn by little boys.

1845. Boy in large turn-down
soft collar

When they had outgrown the age for wearing dresses, boys wore trousers of varying styles and lengths according to their age. From the 1860s they were quite narrow, but became fuller towards the 1890s, just as the fashions for adults changed. The trousers could be gathered on to a waistband.

Small boys were now dressed in short knee length trousers, although pleated skirts or kilts were still to be seen on boys up to the age of about six. Popular from the 1860s until the early 1900s were knickerbockers that were full, but tight fitting at the knees. By the 1870s they became less full, similar in style to knee breeches, and by the 1880s they became like short trousers. Knickerbockers were first worn with short collarless jackets, and the older boys also wore waistcoats.

For holiday wear knitted jersey suits were popular for both their practicality and warmth. Tam-o'-shanters or caps were often worn with these.

Little Lord Fauntleroy dress The book *Little Lord Fauntleroy* by Mrs Frances Hodgson Burnett (1849-1924) inspired boys' fashion around

Plate 3   Eighteenth century. Marionettes 'a la Planchette'

Here can be seen a different form of street entertainment. From abroad came the show with two puppets which were made to move by a single string attached from a fixed post through the figures to the leg of the showman. By moving his leg, the manipulator was able to create the most amazing movements, these being synchronised with the music that accompanied the performance. Seen here the showman is playing the earlier type of bagpipes.

The boy standing on the left is wearing a close fitting coat with the front sloping away to the sides and fastened with buttons. The coat has a turned down flat collar and no lapels. Neckwear was usually just a black ribbon. The waistcoat was short to the waist and the breeches were close fitting. Light coloured stockings were worn. The three cornered hat could be worn cocked in various styles, the hair is smoothed back to form a small queue at the back and tied with a black ribbon. He is seen here carrying a shuttle-cock bat.

The boy in the foreground is perhaps a typical street urchin of this period. His clothes were adaptations of the earlier part of the century and are cut down to fit. The faded red full skirted coat had pocket flaps and turned back cut down cuffs. The waistcoat seen here is worn over the coat and was also cut down to reach the waist. The breeches are full and reach below the knees. Neither shoes nor stockings are worn. His hair is long and unkempt, a three cornered hat being perched on top of his head.

The boy in the centre, although seemingly grown-up by his attire, rides a cock-horse. Following the fashion of his elders he wears the cutaway tail coat. Waistcoats were waist length and cut straight at the bottom, usually double-breasted and sometimes, as in the illustration, with a standing collar. His neckwear is a ruffed shirt front. His breeches are close fitting and cut high to the waist. Striped stockings were fashionable and popular and leather shoes with square or oval buckles were also worn. The tall crowned beaver hat with a wide brim was also very popular.

The small girl is wearing a closed robe, riding coat style, with long close fitting sleeves. The neckline is surrounded by a short cape. The full skirt is encircled at the waist by a wide ribbon tied at the back in a large bow. Beaver hats, similar to the male fashions, were worn decorated with feathers and large bows. Hair was allowed to be natural and curly.

The older girl wears a full skirted gown with the back supported with pads. The close fitting bodice with lace has elbow length sleeves with pleated frills hanging down. The rounded neckline is filled in with a draped muslin neckerchief. A long plain apron with furbelows of lace is also shown. The large muslin hat with a wide brim is decorated with ribbon with a smaller cap worn beneath.

Circa 1864   The very popular Scottish style is demonstrated in this little boy's outfit. He wears a Glengarry cap. The tartan sleeveless waistcoat reveals the full sleeves of the blouse beneath

Circa 1846   This child is in High-land clothes with a plaid over the shoulders. A sporran is attached to the buckled belt. The socks match the tartan kilt. The shoes are buckled

Circa 1870   A plain jacket is worn over the kilt

1886 in the style of a cavalier or Van Dyke — a black velvet suit. This became very fashionable for party wear from the end of the 1880s. These suits had short velvet tunics with large white deep lacey collars and cuffs. The knickerbockers had wide sashes with the ends hanging to one side. Hair was worn long and large plumed hats were also popular with the 'Lord Fauntleroy' fashions.

Plate 4   Nineteenth century, The organ grinder man

Street musicians always gathered around them children of all classes. The small hand organ and the monkey on his shoulder attracted his audience. The little girl in the centre is wearing a hand-me-down shapeless garment. The boy on the left is dressed in a sailor suit. The loose white blouse has a large sailor type collar. The knickerbocker trousers are worn with black woollen stockings and ankle boots. He has a large straw hat, a replica of the real sailor's hat at that time.

The schoolboy in the centre is wearing an Eton suit with a mortar-board type hat. A wide starched collar and bow tie complete the uniform. The older boy wears a short jacket as worn by all classes. The high double-breasted waistcoat matches the coat. A stiff turned down collar with a tie was also worn. The trousers are straight and fairly narrow. Hair was usually worn short.

The girl on the right wears a below-the-knee length full skirted dress. The bodice, with a high neckline, is pleated to the waist, and a wide sash is also worn. The hip length jacket has long lapels and elbow length sleeves. The wide brimmed hat is of straw and decorated with ribbon bows. Buttoned gaiter type boots are worn over black stockings.

Circa 1866 Knickerbockers were popular for little boys around seven years old

Circa 1862 The little boy wears a loose jacket and short trousers

Circa 1863 The little boy is holding a boater style hat and walking stick. The long tunic is worn over pantalettes

Sailor dress In the first quarter of the century boys began to wear sailor type trousers, although knee breeches were still in vogue.

One popular and comfortable fashion was known as a *sailor costume* consisting of a short jacket worn over an open-necked blouse and waistcoat and long breeches. Also very popular again from the 1860s were the sailor suits which comprised blouses with deep flat square collars with a V necked opening at the front, knickerbockers and sailor type hats.

Sailor caps as well as sailor blouses with skirts were also worn by girls. They had various names such as 'Middy suits', 'Jack Tar suits', 'Man-of-War', etc. By the end of the nineteenth century sailor suits were the height of fashion for both small boys as well as girls. Boys wore long trousers whilst girls wore a skirt, usually kilted with a tunic and sailor collar. For summer wear the outfits were of linen, whilst for winter they were made of serge or flannel. Around 1873 three-quarter length trousers were worn with sailor suits with the bloused tops.

Only the wealthier could afford all these fashions. The poorer children very often went bare-footed and were dressed in second-hand clothes.

Circa 1876 This was a typical sailor suit of the period worn with half boots with inside lacings

Towards the end of the 1800s boys from the age of around five wore short trousers that ended at the knees. Short socks were also worn, leaving the knees bare. The sailor suits were still popular and had flat turned-over collars and the tops were bloused. These were worn with short trousers by little boys, whilst girls wore pleated skirts. Sailor-type hats were popular for both boys and girls.

Around 1884 small boys were still sometimes dressed in female clothing, making them look like little caricatures.

School dress Small boys wore a variety of jacket styles with either trousers or knickerbockers. Young boys wore single- or double-breasted jackets, and waistcoats were not unusual. Eton College, the Public School, had a distinctive uniform consisting of a short jacket and a waistcoat made

Circa 1857   This little boy's dress is trimmed with braid and buttoned down the front with mother-of-pearl buttons

Circa 1890   The little boy, still dressed in skirts wears a pinafore. His shoes are laced and he is wearing knee high socks

of vicuna, and striped trousers. Eton-type suits were always very fashionable. The jackets were single-breasted, wide lapelled and fairly short with square cut fronts in red or blue until 1820 when King George III died and the jackets were from then on always black.

Apart from Eton College itself, where the backs of jackets were cut straight, they could often be made with the centre slightly pointed. The lapels were generally deep. The jacket styles were reminiscent of Hussar styles. Waistcoats were worn. Shirts had wide stiff turned-down collars. Before 1820 pantaloons or knee breeches became more popular than the grey trousers that had been fashionable.

Older boys wore Eton-style clothes: long trousers, short jackets and waistcoats. The white shirts worn with this type of outfit had flat collars.

Outdoor dress   Ulsters, chesterfields and inverness capes were the main outdoor wear. Reefer jackets, from the 1870s, were double-breasted with lapels and were worn with knickerbockers by young boys, they could also serve as overcoats. Blazers, from the 1880s, and still popular a century later, were then of flannel, usually striped in club or school colours and worn for sporting events. They had patch pockets.

Headwear and hairstyles   Small boys wore their hair long in curls which were cut short as soon as they began to wear trousers.

For headwear top hats and sailor hats were worn. Peaked and quartered caps were popular as well as knitted stocking caps. For town wear, even very young boys wore bowler hats from the 1860s. Floppy berets or soft peaked caps were also worn, the headwear being similar to that of adults. Their hat styles developed in the same manner as their parents'. Felt hats also became popular.

In the mid 1850s little boys of about six or seven might wear a hat with crowns that were round, made of felt with turned-up brims at the sides, and a cord around the hat tied at the back with two tassels hanging down. Round brimmed hats with ribbon band decoration were worn by boys as well as girls. Very small boys also wore ornamental bonnets. Older boys could wear caps (similar in look to tam-o'-shanters) with peaks and tassels hanging down the side.

Hard peaked caps remained popular among students until about the 1850s. Hats in place of bonnets became the mode around 1862. Boater hats also became popular. In the 1850s boys wore straw hats with streamers or ribbons like the girls, or else they wore caps with coloured or plaid bands. In the later part of the century soft peaked caps became popular. These had earlier been worn by the working classes only. Public school boys wore top hats like their fathers.

When sailor suits were popular for small boys in the 1890s the hats worn with them resembled those of the coastguards, and were made of felt or straw with a ribbon band around the crown and streamers hanging down behind. These were not the same as the sailor hats that became popular a little later.

At the end of the century small boys wore round hats trimmed with ribbon bows and tied under the chin. The brims were generally turned up. Ruching of lace was very popular beneath the brim, framing the hair.

Footwear and legwear   White cotton stockings were popular with boys and girls until the middle of the century, after which time striped and

Circa 1894   This sailor suit was worn with striped socks and long gaiters over the shoes. The trousers were three-quarter length and decorated with buttons. The sailor cap had a ribbon band with short streamers hanging down the back and on top of the centre of the crown was a pom-pon

Circa 1897   The boy is wearing a short reefer jacket with long trousers and spats over his shoes

woollen ones were also worn. Socks at first were only worn by the very young.

In the 1820s shoes often had side gussets, the front being overlapped and buttoned. The *vamp*, which could be of a different colour to the shoe, was often decorated with ornamental stitching. During the latter part of the 1800s children who worked in the mills, wore clogs, a development of pattens. The clogs had wooden soles with iron edging around the soles and heels, and a thick sturdy leather was nailed to this for the uppers.

From the mid-century children's boots could have an elastic gusset on the outer side, and the vamps decorated with appliqué designs in contrasting colours. The shape of the boots was generally square and shallow-toed.

Flat soled slippers with a retaining strap were usually worn indoors, whilst for outdoor wear elastic-sided ankle-high shoes were popular. Shoes were of black glazed leather, and gaiters were worn; these were made of soft chamois. Black or brown laced shoes were also popular worn with ribbed stockings in the Victorian times.

Occupational dress   Victorian boy fishermen wore wide ankle length trousers and woolly jumpers over which were very often worn horizontally striped waistcoats.

Children working in textile and spinning workshops in the mid 1800s wore long pinafores tied at the back, they were usually short sleeved and would be worn over their normal day clothes.

From the mid-nineteenth century page boys' livery suits consisted of tight jackets reaching the waist, similar to that of an Eton College jacket, and pantaloons or long trousers. The tight jackets were invariably padded and always had rows of buttons down the front, often as many as three to five rows, with about eighteen buttons close together on each. Thus the name 'Buttons' became general for this kind of occupation.

Until the 1890s top hats were usual wear, after which date pill-box caps became popular.

Post boys, in the early part of the century wore blue sleeved waistcoats with three rows of gold buttons. One row was used for fastening whilst the others splayed outwards from the centre towards the shoulders for decoration, not unlike a page boy's uniform. Buff coloured breeches and top boots completed the outfit. Brown top hats were also worn. Also fashionable was for the post boys to wear high white beaver hats, blue jackets, red waistcoats with white neckcloths, and short breeches which were often made of white corduroy.

Messenger boys from the 1890s until the late 1950s wore very distinctive pillbox caps, tilted to the right and held on with a chin strap. The uniforms varied very little throughout, except perhaps, in colour. They consisted of military style tunics with a Prussian collar, white metal buttons, a belt and shoulder belt for a pouch to carry messages. The trousers matched the jackets in colour.

In 1851, the year of the Great Exhibition, shoe-black boys were employed mainly from the waifs and strays. They were put into distinctive uniforms of scarlet jackets which were later portrayed by a shoe manufacturer for advertising, and was later worn by men who had licensed pitches for polishing shoes on the streets in London.

Both boys and girls from the age of about six worked in mines. They

Circa 1890   Eton College type outfit with the short jacket and waistcoat. The collar of the shirt was large and flat and lay over the collar of the jacket. A mortar board was generally worn by the boys of Eton College

Circa 1873   Schoolboy in a Victorian style cricket outfit

Circa 1899   Little boy in a round hat with white lace ruching

wore similar apparel to their elders. In the early part of the century they wore very little clothing, just a pair of trousers and a hat. When pulling the wagons along, a chain was attached to the waistbelt. In 1842 a Bill was introduced prohibiting the employment of young children and women from working underground.

Babies

Until about 1900 the less wealthy carried their small children until they could walk, as they were unable to afford baby carriages or prams. At the start of the nineteenth century, until they were about eight month's old, infants' clothes were a little longer than their own length, and as the babies began to walk the clothes were shortened.

Undershirts were still similar to those of the previous century, opening down the front, but made of finer materials such as linen or cambric. The sleeves were similarly set in with a gusset, and were occasionally gathered on to a band at the elbow. The babies of poorer parents wore the upper petticoats and matching frocks in coloured printed designs. The wealthier classes had their frocks of muslin with the upper petticoats of dimity. The skirts of the petticoats were attached to the corset with strings or buttons.

In the first part of the century dresses were generally of a wrap-over style with short bodices and shirt sleeves. Narrow muslin frills and fine embroidery, lace or tucking were the main ornamentation.

A baby's *layette* consisted of a wool body band, a woollen underskirt, a muslin petticoat and a long dress. The dresses, petticoats and cloaks of babies were profusely embroidered and lace edged. Machined tucks and frills became popular with the innovation of the sewing machine (1845). This new invention had a stimulating effect on the decorative aspect of clothing.

Swaddling bands, by now out of favour, were replaced with another type of garment known as a *blanket*. This was made of flannel and worn mainly at night. These gowns were commonly worn from the 1820s with pleats at the waist. The binding was worn over the shoulders and tied with tapes at the back.

Another popular style, to remain until the twentieth century, was a wrap-over style with a tie passing through a slit just beneath the arms and tied at the side.

By the 1820s it was popular for a barrow or flannel square to be wrapped around babies under the arms reaching below the feet where it was turned up and pinned together for warmth. This was still a remainder of the old swaddling clothes, but after this they were completely discarded, and flannel petticoats became the mode.

Shirts, also known as *chemises* from the nineteenth century were still similar to those of previous times, although the sleeve designs altered slightly. The wide gathered sleeves of the first part of the 1800s became very short, sometimes just a small ribbon or lace sufficed with a small gusset at the base of the armhole opening.

The gowns, simple in design at first, became more elaborate with the fashionable puffed sleeve of the 1820s and the 1830s, although by the 1840s sleeves again became shorter and narrower. The bodices became

◀ *Circa* 1859   Little boy with long hair and close fitting cap

▲
Circa 1871   The boy has long bobbed hair and is wearing a sailor blouse. The blue collar is edged with white and has a knotted kerchief

Circa 1869   Boater style hat with a hat band ▶

▲
Circa 1870   Glengarry type bonnet worn by a small boy

longer with more decoration and the skirts also lengthened. A simple gown, popular from the 1820s, similar to the eighteenth century christening robes, was pleated to the waist with straps over the shoulders, or made with hollows for the arms and tied at the back with tapes. Another style fastened with tapes passing through the slits at the sides, a wrap-over variety.

Cloaks or soft woollen shawls were used when the infant was being carried about, and hoods worn over day caps were not unusual. The cloaks were of a circular shape with a collar and sometimes the hood was attached. They were often lined or quilted. In the early part of the century the borders were fringed with silk or edged with swansdown, but later on a quilted edge or embroidered borders also became fashionable.

All babies still wore caps, day and night. These were generally made of either muslin or linen. Plain undercaps with decorative overcaps for day wear that had lace edgings and drawstrings around the head piece were made to adjust for different sizes as the baby grew.

Caps were worn until the 1830s, a popular shape had the crown gathered across the back. This style was known as a foundling shape and was worn for day and night. The poorer children wore caps of soft calico or muslin and these could be of the foundling design, or else a rectangular piece of material shaped with the aid of drawstrings.

Towards the middle of the century the crowns of the decorated or lace caps became quite large with so much trimming that they were then abandoned for indoor wear, but were still seen out of doors. In the late 1870s infants wore *puddings* to protect their heads. These were thick soft rolls of stuffed material tied around the head to protect it from bruises and other injuries. These puddings were popular for many years.

Nightgowns, similar to those worn in the daytime, had long sleeves. Little knitted jackets or *matinée coats*, as they were later called, could be worn over the gowns and beneath capes for extra warmth.

Circa 1885   This little boy dressed as a little girl and with long hair is wearing a Glengarry bonnet and a coat. The lace cuffs, collar and hem of the dress can be seen

Circa 1805   The postboys were dressed in waistcoats with sleeves, and breeches and top hats

Circa 1888   The shoe-black boys with their distinctive red jackets carried their box with shoe cleaning items on their backs like a rucksack

With the advent of new types of baby carriages or perambulators, the fashion for long gowns gradually declined.

Flannel vests began to be worn by babies next to their skin, but towards the end of the century knitted woollen vests were more common.

Swaddling bands still persisted amongst a few, but linen replaced the older type of flannel, and the bands were made shorter and were only wound round the baby twice, until the bands just became binders or knitted bands. Napkins with pins were made safer with a protective shield in 1878, and so were used instead of fastenings with loops and buttons. Over these, *pilches*, often knitted or sometimes made of a waterproof material were worn. Corded bodices or stays were sewn to the petticoats of small infants, but when they reached the age of about two, the bodices were often buttoned together, with an extra row of buttons for the drawers to be attached. Towards the end of the century the chemise and drawers were made in one and were known as combinations. These were usually buttoned between the legs, and were still worn in the early part of the twentieth century.

Knitted cotton or woollen socks or booties were worn to keep the feet warm.

Christening robes   These were profusely decorated with needlework embroidery known as Ayshire work. This was a raised satin stitch with needlepoint filling forming flowers and leaf designs. These robes, much used from the mid 1820s were handed down from generation to generation. The embroidery and shape of the robes worn indicates the period when they were originally made. Christening robes were also made in neo-classical styles as still seen today with a high-waisted Empire line. These were generally pink for girls and blue for the boys.

Toys

In the nineteenth century inexpensive mechanical toys became more numerous. Wind-up and articulated dolls that moved on a cant system were seen as early as the mid 1800s. Talking dolls really only became popular after Thomas Edison invented the phonograph, and a round disc and gramophone mechanism was developed to go inside a doll. Before this, they emitted sounds like 'mama' and 'papa' by means of bellows.

In the nineteenth century educational toys became even more popular, with the Prince Albert among the many parents to encourage this trend.

Gardening toys, carpentry, cookery and chemistry sets were all becoming freely available. Optical toys, for example paper discs with a different picture on each side which when rotated fast, superimposed these images to seem like one, and flicker books worked on the same principle, giving an impression of movement. Magic lanterns and kaleidoscopes were also seen as early as the mid-nineteenth century. There were many such inventions with different names and methods of use. One such was a thaumotrope invented about 1825, which worked a rotating disc.

Toy theatres were also popular throughout the century with cut-out scenery and figures filling the stage.

Glove and string puppets, although not strictly just children's playthings, were extremely popular, expecially when used for Punch and Judy shows and shadow theatres.

Circa 1880　The wooden cart is being pulled along by a horse covered in leather

Circa 1890　Miniature wooden horse and cart with a small doll inside

Circa 1895　This little boy is riding a small bicycle

William Britain was the first to make hollow lead toy soldiers which were very popular by the late nineteenth century.

With the advent of the railway and later the motor car, these also appeared as very popular toys.

Baby dolls or dolls dressed as babies were not available until the 1820s. Before then dolls were all dressed as replicas of the children who in turn were dressed as miniature adults.

As early as Victorian times dolls were being made to look like famous personalities. Golliwogs, in the late part of the century were one of the first mascot toys. A golliwog was a grotesque character in a best selling children's story book.

Circa 1895　A typical Victorian street scene with a street musician playing a bassoon. The little girl in the foreground is wearing a pinafore over her dress. The boy on the left is in a cap, jacket and knickerbockers, whilst the other two boys in the front are dressed in more ragged clothes selling newspapers

Nineteenth century. The baby is swaddled and laid on a long pillow which was folded over the feet to under the chin and tied with wide ribbon bows. This could be placed on a bed or table

Circa 1890 The valance and canopy of the cots in the Victorian times were very decorative

◄ *Circa* 1864 This three month old baby wears a bonnet with a profusion of ruching and bows

Circa 1833 The little boy in a dress is standing by a horse on wheels

Circa 1891 Little boy on a tricycle made with a horse body

Circa 1894 The little girl is holding up a doll dressed in the period, even the high buttoned boots are similar to those worn by the child

The Twentieth Century

Circa 1906   This little three year old boy was still dressed in a pleated skirt and a blazer-like jacket. The large crowned hat was in a sailor style

In the twentieth century children's clothing became simpler in style and was generally designed specifically for them.

Early in the century very small boys and girls wore dresses with high yokes, the full skirts shirred to them. Girls, from about five years wore frilled bonnets, as many as three tiers of frilling framing the face. They were held on by ribbons tied under the chin. The ribbons matched the lining colour of the bonnets. They wore full, long frocks with frills at the hem and also across the yoke as well as at the wrists. Silk stockings were popular. Kid slippers and gloves were also worn.

From about 1908 *bloomers* became more popular than petticoats or drawers.

Until the 1930s toddlers, both boys and girls, wore leggings with matching jackets or coats for outdoor wear. These could be made of knitted stockingette or a warm material. Coats and matching hats were also worn by children to at least the age of five. The Second World War brought with it many restrictions in the way of dress. Trimmings and embroidery were forbidden among a host of other economies: the number of pockets were restricted, pocket flaps were disallowed, as were pleated skirts, turn-ups on trousers, jackets that were double breasted, the number of buttons used and many more.

From 1939 until the 1960s there was barely a change in the designs of garments.

Sweaters, pullovers, jackets, slacks, shorts, all became fashionable after the Second World War. Raincoats were made with removable linings, and many coats were being made of synthetic fur or trimmed with it.

Siren suits, first worn during the Second World War, had attached hoods and fitted cuffs at the wrists and ankles. They were made in a warm, practical and washable material, as not only were they worn in the day-time, but for nights when the children were taken out of their beds and went into shelters during air raids. They were a very practical addition to night attire.

These siren suits became so popular that they were made in a variety of styles, from battledress to more sophisticated fashions. They were not only worn by small children as well as the older ones and grown-ups, but eventually these all-in-one suits were adapted for baby wear. They have remained popular for generations, later becoming known as snow

Circa 1902   This hat has, under the brim, pleated chiffon with lace and ribbon bows arranged over the crown. The coat, also very ornate has a frilled lace edging to the wide shawl collar, and the hem is edged in a deep flounce

Circa 1903   The shirt has a pleated front and a large stiff collar

Circa 1902   A turn-of-the-century outfit. The frilled drawers just peeping beneath the hemline. The yoke is profusely layered in lace

Circa 1904   The little girl wears a very ornate frilled bonnet. Her dress has a large loose collar and the top is shirred. It is belted at hip level

suits among others.

Man-made fibres and synthetics were made to be non-iron and crease-resistant and also with silicone waterproof finishes from the 1950s. These had a great influence on clothes as they were more hard-wearing and could be easily washed and dried, replacing many natural fabrics. They neither shrunk nor changed shape.

With the advent of plastics, there was a revolution in the design of shoes and many other items of apparel and accessories.

In the early 1960s little girls wore fewer chocolate-box style clothes with the smocking and sugary colours. The silhouette was less fussy and more positive. Colours such as red, green and black became fashionable. Instead of the usual white socks, coloured tights became popular. Dress materials also changed; dainty silks and cottons were replaced by corduroy and velvet.

Girls

In the early part of the century dresses were simple, yoked or quite plain. Short dresses with belts at the hips were popular. After the First World War when hand knitting had become so popular, children wore many hand knitted garments like jumpers, cardigans, gloves, hats, scarves. Hand knitted clothes have remained popular throughout the century, even to dresses and skirts, from the 1930s. A style of dress to become extremely popular in the mid 1930s, was a dress worn by the film actress Shirley Temple, and named after her. This was straight and loose fitting with little short puffed sleeves and a falling collar with a shoestring bow at the neck. The dress was very short ending well above the knee. The Shirley Temple curly hairstyle also became world famous.

Pictoral motifs popularised by cartoons were printed or embroidered on many children's clothes from the 1930s.

Quite often the little girls who as yet had no well defined waist wore skirts that were attached to cotton bodices, so that the skirts could hang correctly. Until the little ones started school they were usually dressed in pastel shades, slightly darker than the usual baby colours. The dresses generally had the waist just above the natural line. Peter Pan or pointed collars were very popular.

By the late 1930s summer dresses were usually of cotton, and could be in small checks or stripes. These were often used for school dresses, whilst small floral patterns and spots were for everyday wear. Seersucker, which did not need pressing was also very popular before the non-iron materials came on to the market. The younger children frequently had knickers made of matching materials to their frocks.

Short sleeves were puffed at the shoulders and ended with a small band or cuff. The waistline often had a tie belt of self material. Until the age of twelve the skirts of the dresses were full, gathered to the waist, after which age they were more tailored with slight flares or pleated all round. One or two knife pleats front and back were also seen. Boleros, made popular by the film star Deanna Durban, were often part of an ensemble matching or in contrast to the dress. They could be short sleeved or without any sleeves. Occasionally the boleros were just fronts stitched into the side seams of the dress.

Circa 1904 The bonnet is covered with lace and ruching and the base of the frock is ornamented with broderie anglaise and has a sash at the hips. High boots were still worn

Circa 1905 This litle girl is still dressed in a cumbersome broderie anglaise dress with a ribbon belt passed through slits. Around the neckline is also slotted a ribbon

In the 1930s dress became more tailored and simple in cut. Girls wore classical suits and smarter cut coats.

Costumes or suits became very popular. Short loose jackets or boleros were worn with blouses and skirts or over matching dresses. The jackets often just had a button fastening at the neckline and were allowed to fall open to reveal the garment beneath. Tailored costumes, also very fashionable in the 1930s and 1940s had hip length jackets worn over straight skirts. The jackets were generally single-breasted with long revers and turned back collars.

For winter wear dresses were always in wool with long sleeves. The colours were more definite than those worn in summer, and the material could be checked or woven in various textures. Hand-knitted or machine knitted dresses were also worn. Bobbles and bows as well as frills were used as ornamentation apart from ribbed necklines and cuffs. Machine or hand-knitted jumper suits were extremely popular for all ages. The styles for winter dresses followed those of the summer with full skirts for the younger, and narrower and slimmer styles for the teenagers. Wrist cuffs were buttoned and buttons were also used as decoration down the front to the waistline. The ever popular sailor suit was also being made in knitted materials. The middy top was generally in navy blue with a white collar and the skirt pleated.

Afternoon dresses were still being worn until after the Second World War. These were not too formal, but prettier than the everyday wear. They were worn for Sunday best. Gloves were also worn on these occasions. Party dresses were made of fine materials with hand worked smocking, tucks and pleating. Materials could be of flowered or spotted designs, lighter cotton or voile being used extensively.

Plain collars and cuffs, frills, lace and smocking at the yoke to give extra fullness to the skirts was quite usual.

The more formal party dresses had a profusion of trimmings, such as flowers, ribbons and bows, ruching or embroidery and very full skirts. Georgettes, taffetas, velvets for winter, were materials mainly used. For the very young these dresses ended above the knees.

Twin sets — jumpers and cardigans were worn from the age of five. These were usually quite plain with ribbed necklines, cuffs and welt. The sleeves could be set in or of a raglan type. Fair Isle designs on the yokes of jumpers and cardigans were often seen.

Austerity and wartime controls forebade many extravagances so that dresses became plainer. Matching dress and knicker sets were not allowed to be made above a certain size and the mode for matching knickers never returned.

Blazers and jackets had to be made single-breasted and the numbers of buttons were restricted. Skirts were not allowed to be pleated all round, only a few necessary box or inverted knife pleats were permitted. All these restrictions were enforced to save materials and labour.

Just after the War bib-fronted dresses with insets from the neckline emphasised with either frills or buttons and bows to the waistline with full gathered skirts became very popular. The short sleeves ended just above the elbows, and the skirts ended just below the knees.

To achieve the impression of shoulder width in dresses, a frill tapering in

Circa 1907
Norfolk suit
with breeches

Circa 1911   The skirt of this dress
is gathered on to a high yoke. The
strap and button shoes were worn
with short ankle socks. This style
of dress remained popular for
several decades

Circa 1912   This girl is wearing
a smart coat and hat and is carrying
a small bag. She is wearing gaiters
over her shoes

front to the waist from the shoulders was popular. Sleeves were also padded on the shoulders to give extra broadness.

Pinafore dresses were a practical addition as old dresses could easily be converted and worn over blouses or jumpers.

Around 1946 the shape of skirts altered from the straight pleated kind for teenagers to a very full dirndl skirt style made of straight pieces of material fully gathered on to a wide waistband and made to stand out with layers of frilled stiff petticoats.

Instead of the usual short puffed sleeves, cap sleeves became popular. Also three-quarter length sleeves to just below the elbows were being worn for summer and winter wear. Another very fashionable mode was very full sleeves gathered at the shoulders and caught in a tight fitting cuff at the wrist, very popular on blouses as well as dresses which could be made of any light material, including thin woollens.

For party wear very little girls wore their skirts down to the ankles. Their dresses were often trimmed with ruching. The teenagers usually wore them to mid-calf length, very full with stiffened petticoats beneath. The neckline was often heart shaped with the bodices tight fitting.

The introduction of the New Look in 1947 introduced longer skirt lengths, more rounded shoulders and small waists also became more emphasised. Gored skirts to indoor and outdoor wear helped this illusion. To emphasise the small waist, peplums widened the hips on narrow skirted garments and curved shoulders were achieved with dolman sleeves. The tailored costume, so popular in the 1930s, was replaced by suits with longer jackets buttoning to the neck and flaring out from the waist, which was encircled by a belt.

By the end of the 1950s the princess line was becoming popular, more so than the New Look which had remained in vogue for almost ten years. Chemise or sack dresses with shorter skirts also became very popular, these gave a straight silhouette. This popularised knitted tubular materials, the garments also becoming known as sweater dresses. The cuffs and necklines were ribbed, and the waistline could also be ribbed. When jackets were worn with these dresses they were usually square cut with three quarter length sleeves.

Trapeze shaped dresses were more popular for the younger children, although they also became fashionable for older girls and grown-ups.

Nightwear   Nightdresses were long in the 1930s, but from the 1950s teenagers preferred them shorter, they were made in a wincyette for winter and in cotton fibres for summer, later replaced by flame-proof synthetics.

Outdoor dress   Coats, after the War were still wide shouldered, emphasised with piping from the shoulders tapering to the waist. Previously the emphasis had been achieved with epaulettes and capes, but forbidden due to wartime shortages. The skirts of coats were usually slightly flared. These styles were the same for girls of all ages. Coats which had been fairly straight or slightly flared gradually altered in the late 1940s. Peplums were added to give emphasis on the hips to waisted coats. In the 1950s loose coats known as *swaggers* or *jiggers* became very popular and could be worn over costumes and bulky clothes in the winter. They were also popular for spring and summer wear made in lighter materials. These were

Circa 1917 The party frock is tied around the waist with a ribbon sash and the skirt is flounced at the base

Circa 1927 A simple dress with buttoned shoes and a cloche hat ▼

▲ *Circa* 1927 Dresses became much simpler. This one is decorated around the borders and top with small appliqué flowers. The socks were short and had ribbed tops. The sandal-like shoes had a bar to the strap fastening

made in a variety of styles: with one or two buttons at a yoked neckline, the backs with added gore to give extra swing. Sleeves were often quite wide with deep cuffs. The swagger coats were generally only fastened with a belt or worn loose. The belt could be semi fitted, passing through slits at the side seams or worn completely around the waist. These coats could be full length or just three quarter. Coats, in the 1950s, when worn with the chemise and trapeze line dresses often had deep collars and very large buttons. Half belts at the back were often seen.

Leisure wear By the end of the 1930s, just before the Second World War, clothes for play and holidays, not necessarily just for sport, became a new addition to the wardrobe. Instead of tucking dresses into knickers at the seaside, little girls began to wear *playsuits* — similar to romper suits that babies wore. Boyish tailored shorts were also being worn by boys and girls of all ages. From just after the mid 1940s shirred elastic bathing costumes that fitted all shapes and sizes were made in a great variety of materials and styles. When sun or playsuits first appeared in the 1950s they were one piece garments, the tops sometimes halter-necked or with brief straps over the shoulders with short pleated skirts or shorts attached.

Sun dresses with matching boleros were made with close fitting bodices with strapless tops held up by boning or halter necks. Thin shoulder straps were also seen. Playsuits with similar tops to the sundresses had the lower part very full, like bloomers.

Cardigan jackets were often made to match. Other holiday outfits included wrap-over skirts or open shirts buttoned down the front, worn over shorts. Young children began to wear briefer shorts with play tops for summer wear, the midriff sometimes being left bare.

A great deal of elasticated shirring was used to give a good fit to the bodice and waist. Two piece playsuits and swimsuits also made their appearance in the later 1950s, becoming briefer, then becoming known as *bikinis*. After the War *T-shirts*, first worn in the USA, gradually made their appearance in England. First they were just plain white, short-sleeved tops with rounded necklines, but eventually, because of their simplicity and good value these became so popular that different variations, colours and patterns evolved.

School dress School wear had already begun to alter after the Second World War. The uniforms became simpler in style and instead of the gym slip, pinafore dresses, or skirts and blouses were becoming more popular with V-shaped neck pullovers or cardigans for the winter. Blazers nearly always bore the school badge. Short divided skirts or very short skirts were worn for school games. Straw or panama hats were worn in the summer and velour in winter with school hatbands. By the 1960s headwear was being seen less and less, although for a short while berets with just the school badge were worn.

In the 1930s socks were permitted in the summer, taking the place of thick dark stockings. Even for winter wear the woollen stockings were superceded by lisle and later nylon flesh-coloured stockings.

Headwear and hairstyles Sunday best hats in the summer were made in a variety of straws with floral trimmings or ribbons which were not as long as previously, to form streamers, but just enough to embellish the brims. Boaters were also popular. However these also disappeared gradually in

Circa 1930 Woolly close-fitting cap with a pom-pon at the top

Circa 1930 Playsuit being worn by a little girl, with a soft hat to give protection from the sun.
As can be seen the little girl carries a bucket and spade ready to play in some sand

Circa 1932 Dressed for winter wearing a knitted woolly cap with a pom-pon and matching pullover. The long warm leggings overlap the footwear

the after-war years.

Hoods attached to raincoats were practical and therefore remained in vogue. For winter wear pixie hoods, either knitted or of a woven material became extremely popular for little girls during the War years and by the late 1940s, hoods made to match the coats, came in a variety of materials and were lined in contrasting colours, as well as in tartan.

After the War felt hats became more modish with deeper crowns and off-the-face brims. The poke bonnet-like shapes were being seen less. Wide brimmed hats with small crowns were popular from the 1940s.

Breton sailor type hats with wide off-the-face brims with streamers down the back remained popular for a long time.

In the mid 1950s brimless half-hats became fashionable. These could either be fastened to the hair with slides, or, more usually a spring wire was inserted so that they held on. These hats allowed fashionable pony tails to remain intact, and most hairstyles remained undisturbed.

Also popular in this period were butcher style caps made in eight segments often with a tassel hanging at the back. Some also had small peaks in the front.

Knitted tubes as hats, fitting snugly to the head, were made in a variety of styles, and these usually had matching scarves and gloves.

At the start of the century hair was tied in ribbon bows on either side of the head. Centre partings were very popular. By the 1920s hair styles became shorter, but ribbon bows for the younger ones were so large that it became impractical for headwear to be worn.

Longer hair and pony tails again became very fashionable after the Second World War, as well as hair worn up in the front, and left to hang down long at the back.

Footwear and legwear At the start of the century gaiters were still popular. For winter they were fur lined and made of leather. They fastened under the feet with elastic and fitted right over the shoes and were buttoned up on the outside.

Short ankle socks were worn by the younger girls whilst long cotton or wool socks reaching to just below the knees often had fancy patterns. These latter were for everyday wear, but plain silk was worn for parties and Sunday best. The tops had close ribbing which was meant to support them.

By the Second World War school shoes were sturdy lace-up or buckled styles, usually black or brown.

For summer wear the sandals were similar in style to those worn by boys. Just after the Second World War wedge heeled shoes were popular in all styles including plain court shapes. The variety of leather for shoes improved, suede or grained leather becoming general. Lace-ups and one-bar sandals though were still being worn.

High heels became fashionable for teenagers in the late 1950s. These were very pointed and spikey, known as *stilettos*.

Synthetic fibres introduced in the 1950s made socks much harder wearing. They could be made with stretch yarns to give a better fit.

Seamed stockings were superceded by circular knitted nylons which also stretched. By 1958 nylon tights, which could be made fully fashioned with or without a seam at the back, reached from waist to toe, thus cut-

Circa 1931   This short little frock
has needlework design decoration.
Sturdy lace-up boots were still
being worn to give strength to the
ankles

Circa 1917   The scarf is tucked in
under the half belt at the back of
the coat. The high leggings or gaiters
were buttoned up on the outside

ting out garters and suspender belts.

Boys

Little boys in the early part of the century wore modernised versions of the skeleton suits with shirts buttoned to short trousers. They also had a choice of Norfolk suits worn with trousers or breeches. Eton-style suits or tailored suits like those of the men. From the early part of the century they began to wear flannel, tweed and serge suits. They often wore flat hats or caps with peaks. Little boys wore shorts and blazers as school uniform as well as for every day wear. Day to day wear became more casual. Play and sports wear especially designed for the specific needs of each individual sport was also coming into fashion.

Boys' clothing was rather plain. After the baby clothes they were dressed in short trousers and jackets which could be single- or double-breasted. The jackets were similar to those of adults. Long trousers were not worn until the boys were about fifteen or sixteen years old.

From the mid 1940s very small boys began to wear dungaree type trousers with brace tops or little trousers that were held up with an elasticated waist. This fashion was very soon followed by the little girls as well.

In the 1950s coloured or tartan waistcoats were worn by little boys, especially for parties. Short knee length trousers which until the 1950s were just cut-off versions of long trousers, became more fashionable, becoming shorter and having smarter styling. In the 1950s toddlers began to wear romper suits made of knitted materials, the jackets with lapels and double-breasted fastenings. Cardigans were superceded by collarless middy jackets with brass buttons. Sherlock Holmes type hats with the practical ear flaps were popularised by the then very young Prince Charles.

Shirts lost their tails in the 1950s and were made straight at the base, allowing them to be worn casually outside the trousers and shorts instead of being tucked in.

Chunky sweaters were also making their appearance, and these were knitted or embroidered in a great variety of designs.

The Teddy Boy look made its appearance first in the late 1940s. This was an entirely British mode begun by the teenagers. Their outfits consisted of Edwardian style jackets with high velvet revers and wide padded shoulders. The shirt collars were high and stiff. Elegant waistcoats and long narrow ties were also worn. The trousers were narrow, like drainpipes. The footwear worn with these outfits at first was flat with very thick soles or crepe, later to become more elegant with long pointed toes.

The teenage girl counterparts were usually dressed in tight black skirts and high-necked jumpers. Their jackets were also long, and the high-heeled shoes in the 1950s evolved into winkle-pickers, long pointed toes with long thin heels known as stilettos. These became fashionable with all girls and adults alike in the 1950s.

Occupational dress   Children when working in any trade always wore aprons for the protection of their clothing. Only at the beginning of the twentieth century did overalls come into use. They were also known as *boiler suits*. Some overalls were of the bib and brace variety, still in use at the present time for workmen. They also became popular as children's play wear and actually became a fashion.

Circa 1935   This little girl is wearing a loose comfortable dress and is playing with a yo-yo

In the 1930s corduroys became popular. These were originally worn by working men and farmers, but were very practical for boys as well.

Nightwear   Pyjamas hardly altered for years. The trousers had a narrow drawstring to hold them up, later the waistband became elasticated and a button fastened the front.

Swimwear   In the 1950s swim trunks became very brief, made in satin finishes, and stretch materials, all suitable for swimming, and much better fitting than previously.

Outdoor wear   Rubberised cotton mackintoshes or waterproof gaberdine overcoats were worn in rainy or cool weather and often had matching hats or hoods. These coats were longer than ordinary coats to afford greater protection.

By the early 1950s lumber jackets with welted waists and wrist cuffs were becoming more popular than coats. These jackets reached the hips and were fastened from the neck with zip fasteners or buttons.

Short duffle coats were also found to be more practical than ordinary coats as they were warmer and sturdier.

School dress   In the very early 1900s boys wore school uniforms that were available from specialist shops or large stores. They were, however, becoming less formal. Even in many Public Schools, striped trousers were being replaced by grey shorts for the younger boys and grey flannel trousers for the older ones. More casual lumber jackets or, more often, blazers replaced the more tailored black jackets and waistcoats. These were worn not only as school attire, but also informally. School uniforms were not much different than ordinary everyday wear. Blazers with their patch pockets were like those of the girls' except that the buttoning was in reverse. They always bore the school emblem. School ties in the colours of the school were also worn.

School caps were made in segments which could be in alternating colours of the school with the badge on the front. In summer boaters were worn in Public Schools.

Headwear and hairstyles   Hair was worn short in the 1920s by boys, with short back and sides. In the 1940s and 1950s when the Teddy Boy image was so fashionable, hair was allowed to grow longer than in previous years. The popular style was to have a quiff in the front and the back brushed into a duck's tail.

In the earlier part of the century cotton hats with stitched brims were worn by small boys as a protection against the sun. In 1955 when the film 'Davy Crocket' was first seen, the American frontier style became very popular with small boys, the fur hats especially with their tails hanging down the back became almost a craze.

Footwear and legwear   Elasticated yarn, in the mid 1930s, woven into the ribbed tops of socks obviated the need for garters. Footwear which in the early part of the century was ankle length, buttoned or laced, was becoming lower, being made to fit and give better support in the correct places. Black or brown were favourite colours. Shoes were generally laced up and low heeled. For sports, plimsolls in canvas with rubber soles were worn, indoors as well as out of doors.

Sandals with punched-out designs were worn for the summer. In the late 1950s sandals were made less solid and were mainly wide strapped

Circa 1935   This little girl is wearing a type of dungaree and mob-type hat. Through the upright sandal bar is slotted the fastening strap. She is seen holding a hoop and stick

Circa 1934   School uniform with hat and hatband. Blazers in school colours were very popular. A satchel can be seen carried on the back to hold the school books

Circa 1926   The boy is wearing a school striped blazer and shorts. The quartered cap shows a school badge. The ribbed socks are knee high

Circa 1915   The boy with the short cut hair is wearing a waistcoat beneath the single-breasted blazer. The shoes are of the lace-up variety

Circa 1926   The double-breasted blazer is worn over a shirt and tie and the socks end just above the knees which are visible. The socks are knee high and are turned over at the top

Circa 1920   This little boy is wearing a large soft cap with a brim. The short coat has a fly front hiding the buttons. The high socks reach the knickerbockers

Circa 1907   This schoolboy is wearing a cricket outfit with long trousers with turn-ups, a style that was to remain for some time

Circa 1907   Boy in a sailor outfit of the period with a reefer jacket

Late 1930s Polo necked sweater worn by boys and girls

Late 1930s The hand knitted cardigan had a design of contrasting colour on the pockets and sleeves. These were popular for boys and girls of all ages

Circa 1940 This siren suit is made on a battledress style. The child is wearing a pixie hood, and carrying a gas mask in a box over his shoulders

uppers. Black patent leather pumps were worn for learning to dance and also formal occasions.

Babies

In the first part of the century baby clothes and dress remained long and cumbersome until the child was about eight months old. Flannel binders were still in use.

It was not until the First World War that the long clothes began to get shorter and layettes became more practical, consisting merely of a vest, petticoat and dress.

The vests, usually made of wool could be round necked with a ribbon insertion drawn up to fit around the neckline. Wrap-over styles which tied at the side also became popular. The sleeves were generally short. The flannel petticoats, quite plain, were usually high yoked. Babies' dresses became shorter after they were a few months old to about 60 cm (2 feet) long, or just to cover their feet. The dresses, even worn by little boys in the early part of the century until they were about four, were not as ornate as previously, although frilled edging and a little embroidery was still popular for best wear, becoming simpler in design for everyday.

Most gowns were double yoked, but bibs were still worn. For practicality bibs were of a towelling although the more decorative ones of lighter fabrics were worn with the prettier party dresses, mainly for show.

A great many babies' vests, pilches and other small items were hand-knitted when that became a popular pastime during the First World War. Knitted baby bootees had ribbon insertions around the ankles to keep them on, although little leggings with the feet attached were also worn.

Matinée jackets fastening down the front from the neck with either mother-of-pearl buttons or ribbons were knitted to match the bootees or leggings. Tiny shoes made either of very soft kid or satin with soft soles could also be worn. Large square shawls with a wide border folded in a triangle were used to wrap up babies to keep them warm.

Pram sets comprising bonnets, matinée coats and leggings were always popular for babies wear. Cardigans also became popular after the baby was a few months old. These often had ribbed waists, and the sleeve cuffs were also made close fitting.

As babies began to toddle, leggings instead of having the feet included ended at the ankles, so that shoes could be worn.

By the 1930s babies were permitted to be in the open air in the summer with the minimum of clothing, thus being exposed to the sun. Children, in general began to wear much less in the summer, especially on holiday when sun suits became popular.

When babies reached the crawling stage *romper suits* were the practical answer. These were made in one piece with a high yoke and smocked.

The short legs were elasticated at the thighs and were buttoned under the crotch. Little suits made in two pieces with the bloused top either loose or buttoned to the full bloomer style knickers were also worn.

In the main, romper suits were made of knitted materials, although for the summer cotton was the more usual.

Whilst still in their prams, short artificial silk dresses with smocking and embroidery were worn by boys and girls alike, although boys could

1950s Denim dungarees or blue jeans were worn by boys and girls alike. Check shirts were also popular

wear smocks and blouse knickers. Pastel shades or white were at first the only accepted colours for babies, although nowadays much deeper colours are just as popular.

The matinée jackets that could be worn over dresses from the late 1940s were replaced by more practical cardigans with welted waists, and were fastened across with buttons.

Nightwear For night attire long flanelette nightdresses with long sleeves, either with a cross-over front tied at the side or ribbon tied at the back were worn, later pyjama suits that fastened across the top of the shoulders became more popular.

In the 1950s an entirely new kind of sleepwear was introduced, gradually becoming more popular than any of the previous styles. This was a bag made of a wool and cotton mixture, which allowed babies complete freedom of movement, with the bottom closed, keeping the baby covered at all times, however boisterous.

By the 1950s babies' pants had improved immensely. The leg holes were placed more to the front so that a great deal of unnecessary bulk was eliminated. The back part, especially for baby girls was elaborately trimmed with frills that were visible from beneath the more popular short dresses. Nappy and plastic linings were made to allow air to circulate whilst holding in the moisture — a vast improvement on the older type of rubber pants.

Christening robes These were usually handed down as heirlooms from Victorian times. When new ones were bought, the underslips could be of silk, whilst the robe itself was very lacey. The matching bonnets often had rosettes over the ears and ribbon ties. The gowns were round necked with puffed sleeves, the edges bound in silk. The yoke could have vertical tucks and embroidery. Crêpe-de-chine or net over the silk gown was often used.

In the late 1940s instead of a shawl, a cape with hood attached made in soft wool with lacey designs and trimmed with swansdown was found to be far more practical, and this became the mode, even for everyday wear.

Toys

Teddy bears, first seen in the 1900s, became one of the most popular and fascinating toys for children. They originated in America and were named after President Theodore (Teddy) Roosevelt. Later, in the 1930s, Shirley Temple dolls and many other playthings became by-products of film and cartoon characters.

Meccano, originally called Mechanics Made Easy, was introduced in 1901 by Frank Hornby who also created Hornby trains. These are still amongst the most popular and lasting toys to-day. Indeed constructional toys rate amongst the most popular educational playthings.

Late 1950s The pleated skirt is worn with a plain long sleeved blouse

Glossary of Terms

Aiglettes   tags or metal sheaths. Points used to tie different parts of costume together. They were attached to ribbons or cords. Aiglettes could also be used ornamentally on caps, and on slashings or garments.

Barrow   baby's flannel wrapped around the body and pinned up, covering the feet.

Bearing cloth   cloth or mantle used to cover a baby when being baptised. Usually decorated with lace or a fringe.

Belly-piece   stiffening sewn into the lining of a doublet forming a corset-like ridge down the belly.

Biggin   child's cap or hood, shaped like a coif. *Beguine* meant nun, the word derived from a nun's plain linen cap.

Billiment   decorated border of French hood. The upper billiment decorated the crown and the nether billiment the front edge of the bonnet.

Bliaut   long close fitting tunic, slit at the side and long sleeved.

Bombast   stuffing for clothes, generally cotton and rags, to make them stand out.

Bongrace   pendant flap at the back of a French hood which could be turned up over the crown to protect the face. As a separate item it could be stiffened, covering the head and the back of the head to the shoulders.

Braes   primitive form of drawers, at first an outer garment with wide, loose short legs, held up with a running string through a waist hem.

Breeches   *braccae* in Celtic, upper part of hose, or type of drawers.

Busk   part of dress stiffened with wool or whalebone, plaited or quilted to keep the body straight.

Cambric   fine linen, originally made at Cambrai used for handkerchiefs, cuffs, collars and shirts, mainly in the Elizabethan era.

Cannon or **Trunksleeves**   distended with padding and also sometimes whalebone, narrowing towards the wrist.

Cassock   long loose coat or gown buttoned up the front.

Caul   close fitting cap, network enclosing the hair.

Chaperon   hood made of a soft material.

Chaplet   circular wreath of flowers or jewels worn on the head by both boys and girls.

Chemise   shirt or undergarment.

Chiton   basic tunic of Ancient Greece worn by boys and girls.

Cloakbag breeches   see Venetians.

Clogs   wooden soles held on with straps over the toes. Sometimes they were hinged beneath the instep to facilitate walking.

Chignon   a mass of real or false hair arranged at the back of the head in a cluster of curls or twisted in a bun.

Coif   close fitting plain linen cap, like a baby's bonnet, worn over the ears and tied beneath the chin.

Corset   sleeveless bodice.

Cote-hardie   closs fitting long overgarment.

Crin   stiff horsehair fabric.

Cuir-bouilly   leather boiled in oil to make it hard and durable, used also for armour and commonly in use in the Middle Ages.

Dagging   scalloped and decorated edges.

Dimity   strong linen cloth.

Doublet   previously known as a *gipon*, but after about 1670 a jerkin was, as its name implies, made of double material with padding in between. It was close and tight-fitting with the skirts just below the waistline. The sleeves could be separate and attached to the armholes with ties.

Falling band   stiffened linen collar falling on to the shoulders, edged with lace.

Farthingale   under support of a wide petticoat.

Fillet   strip of material suitable for binding — headband.

Fitchet   vertical placket hole in a skirt.

Fichu   lacey type of scarf knotted around the neck, the ends in front.

Flounce   ornamental gathering on dress, also known as a *frounce*.

Fontange   high headdress also known as Tower or Commode, named after Mlle Fontange who first introduced it into the French Court in 1680. Made of alternate layers of lace and ribbon raised one above the other.

French hood   headdress worn from the reign of Henry VII to Charles I. Small bonnet made on a stiff frame, worn back on the head with the front curving forward to the ears and trimmed with an edging or billiments and a curtain hanging behind.

Frogging cord and tassel trimming across a garment in the military style.

Frock a dress of thin material with a back fastening.

Galoshes low wooden soled overboots fastened with buckles, worn as protection against dirt.

Gamashes loose leggings or overstockings, also high boots worn as protection against dirt.

Garters decorative bands which tied in bows on the outer side of the leg (mainly seventeenth century).

Gipon forerunner of the doublet — close fitting short padded garment worn over a shirt. The sleeves were long and tight, and fastened on the outer side to the elbows. The front fastening was with buttons or lacing.

Gown the name is derived from the ancient British 'gwn' or Norman 'gunna'. Loose outer garment with wide hanging sleeves, or an overgarment open down the front worn by older children.

Guimp short chemise of a light material to cover the neckline of an open dress. Also a cotton blouse trimmed with lace or embroidery.

Himation long rectangular cloak worn by boys and girls.

Houppelande long voluminous upper garment with long wide sleeves.

Jerkin jacket worn over a doublet which it resembled, with the skirts slightly longer.

Kerchief headcloth.

Kirtle in the sixteenth century a gown and kirtle formed a complete dress, the kirtle worn under a gown as an undergarment was a loose tunic or gown with sleeves and gradually became a skirt or petticoat.

Knightly girdle decorative belt made of metal clasps joined and fastened with an ornamental metal buckle.

Leading strings seventeenth and eighteenth century, long narrow strips of material attached to the back of the armhole like hanging sleeves, used to control small children when walking.

Leg-o-mutton sleeve full at the shoulders narrowing towards the elbow and tight at the wrist.

Liripipe pendant streamers or tails to a hood.

Loo mask half mask just covering the face to the nose.

Manchette ornamented cuff retaining the meaning of the word sleeve from the Latin *manus*. Lace ruffle around the wrist.

Miniver white weazel fur.

Muckinder linen square used as handkerchief worn at the girdle and attached by a tape.

Nankeen woollen cloth in its natural colour, originally from Nankeen in China.

Panes slashed or ribbon-like pieces of material joined top and bottom, allowing for contrasting material to be pulled through.

Pantalettes children's version of ankle length pantaloons showing beneath the dress.

Partlet bodice fill-in with collar.

Pattens thick wooden soles roughly made to the shape of the foot and mounted or tied on a round or oval ring of iron, so that the foot is raised about 2 in. (5 cm) from the ground. The heel is held on with buckles and straps, with a strap over the toes as well.

Peplum rectangle of cloth with the top folded down and pinned at the shoulders.

Phrygian cap or bonnet. Roman headwear made of felt or leather and fastened beneath the chin.

Piked shoes long pointed shoes, the points extending beyond the toes.

Pipkin small flat hat decorated with a jewelled hat-band and feathers.

Plastron front panel of a bodice or blouse in a contrasting colour from the remainder of the garment.

Points ties decorated at the ends with aiglettes that could be used instead of buttons as a form of fastening.

Pomade hair lubricant or hair oil.

Pudding thick roll or cushion stuffed with wool or other soft filling, tied around the head of a little child for protection against knocks.

Puffs shirt or lining protruding through slashes or gaps.

Quarter back part of upper part of shoe which covers the heels.

Queue a hanging tail of hair at the back of the head, sometimes plaited into a pig-tail.

Rabato support for ruffs worn around the neck.

Rapier light sword.

Ruffles pleated frill edged with lace.

Slashings slits in a garment, symetrically designed, allowing for under-garments or linings to protrude.

Slops wide knee breeches or bombasted trunk hose.

Smock girl's garment, sometimes embroidered with coloured silks.

Smocking honeycomb effect achieved by stitching in close gathers.

Spanish hose similar to cloakbag breeches and Venetians. High waisted and pleated at the waist, narrowing towards the knees. They were hooked to the doublet linings and closed with buttons.

Stirrup hose similar to boot hose, but without soles, and held down with an inset strap, made of coarse material, worn over understockings.

Stomacher ornamental chest covering for a front opening of a doublet or bodice, richly decorated in the Elizabethan time.

Swathebondes swathes of cloth in which babies were wrapped, similar to the Egyptian mummies.

Tabard type of jacket or sleeveless coat with the sides left open.

Tippet pendant streamers.
Trunk hose wide breeches.
Vamp upper part of shoe covering the front part of the foot.
Venetians early form of knee breeches, pear shaped and bombasted round hips, tied at the base with points or ribbons.

Vicuna very soft woollen cloth, also known as *melton*.
Virago sleeve puffed and tied with slashings.
Wings projections or welts on shoulders set over the place on top where the sleeves and body of garment are joined.
Whisk very broad collar falling to the shoulders, plain or lace edged.

Bibliography

Amphlett, Hilda, *Hats*, Richard Sadler 1974

Blum, S, *Victorian Fashions and Costumes from Harpers Bazaar 1867-1898*, Dover 1974

Brooke, Iris, *English Children's Costume since 1775,* A & C Black

Brooke, Iris, *English Costume 1900-1950*, Methuen 1951

Buck, A, *Victorian Costume and Costume Accessories*, Jenkins 1961

Cassin-Scott, Jack, *Costume and Fashion*, 2 Vols, Blandford 1975

Contini, M, *Fashion*, Crescent 1965

Cooke, P C, *English Costume*, Gallery Press 1968

Cunnington, C W & Buck, A, *Children's Costume in England*, A & C Black 1965

Cunnington, C W & P, *Handbook of English Mediaeval Costume*, Faber 1969

Cunnington, C W & P, *Handbook of English Costume in the Sixteenth Century*, and *Handbook of English Costume in the Nineteenth Century*, Faber 1970

Cunnington, C W & P E & Beard, C, *Dictionary of English Costume*, A & C Black 1965

Cunnington, P & Lucas, C, *Occupational Costume in England*, A & C Black 1976

Davenport, Milla, *Book of Costume*, Crown Publishers Inc 1972

Ewing, E, *History of Children's Costume*, Batsford 1977

Fairholt, F W, *Glossary of Costume in England*, E P Publishing 1976

Fraser, Antonia, *History of Toys*, Weidenfeld & Nicolson 1966

Garland, Madge, *The Changing Face of Childhood*, Penguin

Garland, M & Anderson-Black, J, *A History of Fashion*, Orbis 1973

Pictorial Encyclopedia of Fashion, Hamlyn 1968

Hansen, H H, *Costume Cavalcade*, Methuen 1960

Jackson, Margaret, *What they Wore, A History of Children's Dress*, Allen & Unwin 1936

Laver, James, *Children's Fashions in the Nineteenth Century*, Batsford 1953

Laver, James, *Costume*, Batsford 1962

Laver, James, *Concise History of Costume*, Thames & Hudson 1963

Laver, James, *Nineteenth Century Costume*, HMSO 1947

Laver, James, *Victorian Vista*, Hulton Press 1954

Lister, Margot, *Costume*, Herbert Jenkins 1967

Moore, D Langley, *The Child in Fashion*, Batsford 1953

Powell, Rosamond Bayne, *The English Child in the Eighteenth Century*, Murray 1939

Remise, J & Fondin, J, *The Golden Age of Toys*, Patrick Stephens 1967

Roe, F Gordon, *The Georgian Child*, Phoenix House 1961

Roe, F Gordon, *The Victorian Child*, Phoenix House 1959

Schorsch, A, *Images of Childhood*, Mayflower Books 1979

Strutt, Joseph, *A Complete View of the Dress and Habits of the People of England*, H C Bohn 1842

Turner Wilcox, R, *Dictionary of Costume*, Batsford 1970

Von Boehn, Max & Fischel Dr O, *Modes and Manners* (8 Vols), Harrap 1926-35

Yarwood, Doreen, *Outline of English Costume*, Batsford 1970

Index

Accessories 13, 20, 33, 38, 30, 47, 59
Apron 18, 20, 23, 26, 27, 28, 34, 35, 39, 47

Babies 11, 16, 22, 30, 36, 53, 67
Barbette 10
Bearing cloth 11
Beret 21, 43, 51, 62
Bib 18, 23, 31, 36
Biggin 18, 22
Billiment 18, 19
Bliaut 11
Blouse 29, 40, 43, 50, 61, 62
Bluecoat boys 21
Bodice 18, 19, 20, 26, 34, 36, 39, 40, 47, 53, 55, 59, 61, 62
Bongrace 19
Bonnet 11, 15, 19, 21, 23, 34, 43, 47, 51, 58, 68
Boots 15, 22, 30, 36, 47, 52
Boys 4, 7, 8, 9, 10, 12, 13, 14, 18, 19, 20, 23, 26, 28, 32, 34, 35, 36, 39, 43, 47, 55, 58, 64, 66, 67
Braes 8, 10
Breeches 8, 18, 22, 28, 29, 30, 32, 36, 39, 48, 50, 51, 52
Bustle 40
Buskin 15

Cap 7, 10, 11, 15, 18, 21, 22, 23, 26, 27, 28, 29, 30, 31, 35, 36, 37, 43, 46, 48, 50, 51, 52, 54, 63, 65
Cape 7, 13, 30, 51, 54, 61, 68
Caul 19
Chaplet 10, 13, 14
Chemise 8, 14, 26, 53, 55, 61, 62
Chiton 4
Christening robes 11, 16, 30, 31, 36, 54, 55, 68
Cloak 4, 8, 9, 13, 16, 19, 27, 29, 34, 47, 53, 54
Coat 19, 22, 29, 32, 35, 36, 58, 60, 61, 62, 63, 65
Codpiece 15, 22
Coif 11, 12, 14, 15, 18, 19, 21, 22, 27, 28
Corset 19, 32, 34, 40, 53
Cote-hardie 9, 12
Crespine 9, 10
Crinoline 39, 40, 47

Doublet 13, 14, 15, 20, 21, 22, 26, 28, 29, 30
Drawers 9, 13, 40, 43, 47, 55, 58
Dress 7, 11, 12, 14, 18, 22, 26, 27, 29, 31, 34, 36, 39, 40, 47, 48, 53, 58, 59, 60, 61, 62, 66

Eton boy 50, 51, 54

Farthingale 18, 19, 27
Fontange 28
Footwear and legwear 10, 12, 13, 15, 19, 22, 29, 36, 47, 51, 63, 65

Garters 22, 26, 30, 64, 65
Gipon 13, 15
Girls 4, 8, 9, 11, 12, 14, 18, 26, 27, 31, 32, 34, 36, 39, 47, 50, 51, 52, 55, 58, 59, 66, 68
Gloves 13, 22, 27, 30, 58, 59, 60
Gown 7, 8, 9, 11, 12, 14, 15, 18, 19, 20, 21, 27, 28, 34, 35, 36, 53, 54, 55, 68
Gunna 7

Hair 4, 7, 8, 9, 10, 11, 12, 13, 14, 15, 19, 21, 28, 29, 34, 35, 43, 47, 49, 51, 63, 65
Hat 15, 21, 22, 28, 29, 30, 35, 43, 47, 49, 50, 51, 52, 53, 58, 59, 62, 63
Hatband 22, 29, 43, 62
Headwear and hairstyles 9, 10, 12, 13, 14, 15, 19, 21, 27, 29, 34, 35, 43, 51, 62, 65
Hood 13, 15, 19, 27, 30, 54, 63, 68
Hose 8, 10, 13, 15, 21, 22, 29, 30
Houppelande 14, 15

Jacket 20, 21, 29, 32, 34, 35, 36, 39, 47, 48, 50, 51, 52, 58, 60, 61, 65
Jerkin 20, 21, 22, 29

Kirtle
Knickerbockers 48, 49, 50, 51
Knightly girdle 13

Leading strings 20, 26, 27, 29
Leggings 30, 36, 66
Leisure wear 62
Liripipe 13
Little Lord Fauntleroy 48, 49

Matinée coat 54, 66, 68
Mantle 11, 13, 19

Nightdress 61, 68
Nightgown 19, 21, 27, 54
Nightwear 61, 65, 68

Occupational dress 30, 36, 52, 64
Outdoor dress 12, 13, 19, 27, 29, 51, 61, 65

Palla 4
Panier 34

Pantelettes 39, 40, 43, 47
Patten 15, 52
Peplum 4
Petticoat 18, 19, 20, 23, 26, 27, 29, 31, 32, 34, 35, 36, 40, 53, 55, 58, 61, 67
Pinafore 14, 27, 39, 47, 52
Pinner 35
Polonaise 34
Pumps 22, 26, 30, 66

Ruff 18, 19, 27, 29

Sailor dress 34, 39, 40, 43, 50, 51, 60
School dress 35, 50, 62, 65
Shawl 11, 31, 54, 66, 68
Shirt 8, 9, 10, 13, 20, 22, 31, 34, 36, 40, 47, 51, 53
Shoes 8, 12, 13, 15, 16, 18, 19, 22, 26, 30, 34, 36, 47, 52, 59, 63, 65, 67
Shorts 10, 58, 62, 65
Skirt 7, 9, 14, 18, 19, 20, 28, 29, 31, 32, 34, 36, 40, 43, 47, 48, 50, 54, 58, 59, 60, 61, 62, 64
Slops 18, 22
Socks 50, 52, 55, 59, 62, 63, 65
Stockings 8, 22, 26, 30, 32, 36, 47, 51, 58, 62, 63
Stomacher 15, 19, 26, 35
Suit 20, 49, 59, 60-7
    boiler 64
    jersey 48
    jumper 60, 61
    Norfolk 64
    romper 67
    siren 58
    skeleton 35, 64
    tunic 47
Surcote 9, 11, 12
Swaddling clothes 11, 16, 22, 30, 31, 36, 53, 55
Swimwear 65

Tabard 15
Tam-O-Shanter 43, 48
Tights 59
Toga 4
Toys 4, 8, 10, 11, 23, 31, 37, 55, 68
Trousers 7, 34, 35, 43, 47, 48, 50, 51, 52, 53, 58, 64, 65
Tunic 4, 7, 8, 9, 10, 11, 12, 13, 14, 47, 49, 50, 52

Veil 4, 10, 12, 14

Waistcoat 20, 27, 29, 34, 35, 36, 39, 48, 50, 51, 52, 65
Watteau gown 34
Wig 29, 31, 34, 35